P9-CKA-808

LITURGY

Sacrosanctum Concilium

REDISCOVERING VATICAN II

Series Editor: Christopher M. Bellitto, Ph.D.

Rediscovering Vatican II is an eight-book series in commemoration of the fortieth anniversary of Vatican II. These books place the council in dialogue with today's church and are not just historical expositions. They answer the question: What do today's Catholics need to know?

This series will appeal to readers who have heard much about Vatican II, but who have never sat down to understand certain aspects of the council. Its main objectives are to educate people as to the origins and developments of Vatican II's key documents as well as to introduce them to the documents' major points; to review how the church (at large and in its many parts) since the council's conclusion has accepted and/or rejected and/or revised the documents' points in practical terms; and to take stock of the council's reforms and paradigm shifts, as well as of the directions that the church appears to be heading.

The completed series will comprise these titles:

Ecumenism and Interreligious Dialogue: Unitatis Redintegratio, Nostra Aetate by Cardinal Edward Cassidy

The Church and the World: Gaudium et Spes, Inter Mirifica by Norman Tanner, SJ

The Laity and Christian Education: Apostolicam Actuositatem, Gravissimum Educationis by Dolores Leckey

Liturgy: Sacrosanctum Concilium by Rita Ferrone

Scripture: Dei Verbum by Ronald Witherup, SS

The Church in the Making: Lumen Gentium, Christus Dominus, Orientalium Ecclesiarum by Richard Gaillardetz

Evangelization and Religious Freedom: Ad Gentes, Dignitatis Humanae by Jeffrey Gros and Stephen Bevans

Religious Life and Priesthood: Perfectae Caritatis, Optatam Totius, Presbyterorum Ordinis by Maryanne Confoy, RSC

LITURGY

Sacrosanctum Concilium

Rita Ferrone

Paulist Press
New York/Mahwah, NJ

The Scripture quotations contained herein are from the New Revised Standard Version: Catholic Edition Copyright © 1989 and 1993, by the Division of Christian Education of the National Council of the Churches of Christ in the United States of America. Used by permission. All rights reserved.

Cover design by Amy King

Book design by Celine M. Allen

Copyright © 2007 by Rita Ferrone

All rights reserved. No part of this book may be reproduced or transmitted in any form or by any means, electronic or mechanical, including photocopying, recording, or by any information storage and retrieval system without permission in writing from the Publisher.

Library of Congress Cataloging-in-Publication Data

Ferrone, Rita.
    Liturgy : Sacrosanctum Concilium / Rita Ferrone.
        p. cm. — (Rediscovering Vatican II)
    Includes bibliographical references and index.
    ISBN-13: 978-0-8091-4472-3 (alk. paper)
    1. Vatican Council (2nd : 1962-1965). Constitutio de sacra liturgia. 2. Catholic Church—Liturgy. I. Title.
    BX8301962.A45C645 2007
    264'.02—dc22
                                                                2007026043

Published by Paulist Press
997 Macarthur Boulevard
Mahwah, New Jersey 07430

www.paulistpress.com

Printed and bound in the
United States of America

CONTENTS

ACKNOWLEDGMENTS

I owe a debt of gratitude to those who have helped me in the course of writing this book. I am grateful to the editor of this series at Paulist Press, Christopher Bellitto, whose vision and unfailing support made this project possible. I am likewise much indebted to Paul Turner, Michael Witczak, and Robert Duggan, who read the entire manuscript and contributed many useful suggestions. Thanks also go to James Schellman, Eliot Kapitan, Lisa Tarker, Vicki Klima, Michael Joncas, Michael Novak, Roger Evans, and Linda Gaupin for clarifications and help with specific questions, and to the Salzman library of Saint Francis Seminary, the library of St. Joseph Seminary, Dunwoodie, and the Fordham University libraries. Finally, I wish to thank my husband, Philip Swoboda, whose brilliant mind and keen editorial eye have helped me on many occasions.

There are other people too whose inspiration and example have been invaluable to me. Without knowing it, they have helped me to write this book. I think in a special way of my teacher, Aidan Kavanagh, OSB, who died as this manuscript was going to press. One memory stands out in particular. I had written to him after hearing him deliver an insightful and challenging address to a large gathering at the first convocation of the North American Forum on the Catechumenate in 1986. I thanked him for "cutting through the confusion" surrounding so many issues in which we were then immersed. His reply was unforgettable. After some gracious words, he wrote the following: "As for confusion, it comes with life. But there are two kinds of confusion, the kind that is life-giving, and the kind that destroys or bemuses. Go for the first, and learn how to spot the second. Then tell the truth. You may not convert the world, but at least you will be able to live with yourself, and remain faithful. God bless your efforts." As I think back over the work of writing this book, I can think of no better way to express what I have tried to do here. It is for the reader to judge how well I have succeeded.

As someone who was born at the end of the "baby boom" generation, I grew up with the Second Vatican Council. It has shaped my understanding of what it means to be Catholic. The implementation of its liturgical reforms is something I have also been privileged to share in my professional life, in venues as diverse as the Archdiocese of New York, the Diocese of Allentown, and the cathedral in Milwaukee—not to mention the many dioceses I have had occasion to visit as a speaker, educator, and consultant over the past twenty years. The work of researching and writing this book, however, has allowed me to step back from the fray, and to both see the great progress the church has made and hear how the Constitution on the Sacred Liturgy continues to call us to deeper fidelity. For this, I am especially grateful.

I dedicate this book to my mother, Wilma Ferrone (1914–1998), who, like so many Catholics around the world, welcomed the reforms of Vatican II.

ABBREVIATIONS

Documents of Vatican II

AA	*Apostolicam Actuositatem* (Apostolate of the Laity)
AG	*Ad Gentes* (Missionary Activity)
CD	*Christus Dominus* (Bishops)
DH	*Dignitatis Humanae* (Religious Freedom)
DV	*Dei Verbum* (Revelation)
GE	*Gravissimum Educationis* (Christian Education)
GS	*Gaudium et Spes* (The Church in the World of Today)
IM	*Inter Mirifica* (Means of Social Communication/Mass Media)
LG	*Lumen Gentium* (The Church)
NA	*Nostra Aetate* (Non-Christian Religions)
OE	*Orientalium Ecclesiarum* (Eastern Catholic Churches)
OT	*Optatam Totius* (Priestly Formation)
PC	*Perfectae Caritatis* (Religious Life)
PO	*Presbyterorum Ordinis* (Ministry and Life of Priests)
SC	*Sacrosanctum Concilium* (Liturgy)
UR	*Unitatis Redintegratio* (Ecumenism)

Other Abbreviations

DD	*Dies Domini*
ELLC	English Language Liturgical Consultation
GDC	*General Directory for Catechesis*
ICEL	International Commission on English in the Liturgy
ICET	International Consultation on English Texts
LA	*Liturgiam Authenticam*

LI	*Liturgicae Instaurationes*
MD	*Mediator Dei*
PP	*Princeps Pastorum*
RCIA	*Rite of Christian Initiation of Adults*
RS	*Redemptionis Sacramentum*
SS	*Spiritus et Sponsa*
SP	*Summi Pontificatus*

PART I

THE DOCUMENT

In order to understand the Constitution on the Sacred Liturgy, three essential pieces of background must be grasped. The first is the general condition of the liturgy in the nineteenth and early twentieth centuries. The second is the role of the liturgical movement in reviving interest in the liturgy as a focus of pastoral concern. The third is the reforms of the liturgy undertaken immediately prior to Vatican II.

After exploring these three areas, we will conclude with a brief summary of the process by which the Constitution on the Sacred Liturgy was produced.

BACKGROUND

1. The Liturgy in Need of Reform

Many aspects of liturgical celebration that Catholics today take completely for granted were lacking in the church of the nineteenth century. In fact, it is one of the marks of the liturgical movement's great success that it now seems to us quite natural to take part in the liturgy with a more or less clear idea of what is going on and with some definite role for the assembly in the prayers and actions of the church's rites.

Regardless of our musical tastes or abilities, it seems normal to us that the congregation is expected to sing certain songs and acclamations that are actually part of the liturgy, such as the Sanctus or the Lamb of God. We generally expect to hear readings and prayers in a language we understand. We are not surprised when the priest says Mass facing the people or preaches on the readings we have just heard. It seems completely normal to us that communion is distributed to the faithful during the communion rite. At the most basic level we expect there to be only one liturgical celebration going on at a time in a given worship space.

None of these matters could be taken for granted in the church of the nineteenth and early twentieth centuries. The priest prayed in a language most of the people did not understand. He said Mass with his back to them, in a voice that for the most part could not be heard, while the people took part in individual devotions autonomously and perhaps sang a few hymns. The choir alone sang the Sanctus and other prayers that now belong to the whole assembly, while the servers alone made the spoken responses. Marriage vows and baptismal promises could be spoken in the vernacular, but nothing else.

There were no missals for the people to "follow along" with what Father was doing, no translations of the Latin for use in the pew, such as existed in the church of the 1940s and 1950s. Such tools were an invention of the liturgical movement, motivated by the desire to have people know what was happening in the liturgy and participate spiritually. Even if you knew the Latin language in those days, chances are you would not have been able to discern what was being said at the average Mass. Many priests themselves were only minimally skilled in pronouncing the prayers, and would mumble or rush through the liturgical texts without any expectation that the people gathered could make head or tail of what was being said. In any case, it was not considered necessary or desirable for them to do so. Attending to the words would be a "distraction" from the individual's prayer.

Sometimes more than one Mass would go on at the same time in the same church, on different altars. Since what the priest was doing didn't have any direct connection to what the people were doing anyway, this didn't necessarily disturb anybody. Concelebration was confined to ordination liturgies; otherwise, each priest said Mass alone.

Preaching was not usually related to the scriptures of the day, even though the Council of Trent had recommended a course of preaching based on the liturgical cycle. Moral exhortation or a talk on some aspect of Catholic teaching was more usual. Because celebrations of the saints could replace the Sunday Mass texts, the seasons of the liturgical year also languished. Lenten liturgies in the month of March could give way to celebrations in honor of Saint Joseph, for example, and the Easter season liturgies that occurred during the month of May could be over-shadowed by celebrations in honor of Mary. Aside from a few weeks during special seasons of the year, there was no weekday lectionary, and many of the rites of the church had no scripture readings assigned to them at all. On Sundays, the lectionary consisted of a single year's worth of readings, not a three-year cycle like the one we have today. Only an epistle and a gospel reading were read. Readings from the Old Testament were rarely heard in church.

The manner in which communion was distributed deserves special notice, because it is so foreign to our practice today. By this I do not mean that it was given on the tongue, or under only one form, or with the communicant kneeling. What really appears strange today is that communion would be given at various times rather than during the communion rite of the Mass itself. Communion was given outside of Mass because it was thought that having the people receive would "interrupt" the Mass. Even as late as 1962, at the Mass that opened the Second Vatican Council, communion was not distributed. Although hundreds of bishops attended, only the presiding minister received. Instead, communion was given out *after* Mass was over. The Austrian liturgical scholar Josef Jungmann, SJ, made a jocular but also some-what bitter remark in his diary at the time that the entire liturgy offered an illustration of how far the church still needed to go in litur-gical reform.[1]

Even in 1905, when Pope Pius X issued a decree urging frequent communion,[2] no attempts were made to put communion into the Mass. Many people received communion more frequently because of the pope's exhortation, but they did so at various times. In his memoir, the Belgian liturgical pioneer Bernard Botte, OSB, recalled that in parish churches during the 1920s communion was given out at fifteen-minute intervals, regardless of where the priest was in the celebration of the liturgy. Sometimes the priest giving communion would actually reach over the priest saying Mass to get hosts out of the tabernacle for this purpose. Botte also told of one woman who was encouraged by her con-fessor to receive communion *before* Mass and then to offer Mass as a thanksgiving![3]

The priests themselves were not well educated in the liturgy. There were no courses in seminaries to study the history, evolution, or structure of the church's liturgical rites. Instead, there were courses on rubrics. Although some historical and spiritual understanding was imparted through such courses, the main focus was on celebrating the rites correctly and thus avoiding sin. No special preparation to teach these courses was required, and consequently various faculty members might take on the task in addition to whatever other responsibilities they had. A survey of French-speaking seminaries taken by the Pastoral Liturgy Center in Paris revealed that most of the teachers of rubrics were bursars.[4] No one knew why. Early in the liturgical movement, some priests responded unenthusiastically to the idea of teaching ordinary people about the liturgy because they assumed this meant studying rubrics, and they knew this would go over poorly, if at all.

Interest in prayer in connection with the liturgy, of course, has never been lacking in the church. But what happened over the course of time, as the liturgy became more remote and inaccessible, was that people prayed *at* Mass. They did not *pray the Mass*. Liturgical theologian Louis Bouyer, in his book *Liturgical Piety*, offered a penetrating critique of what had become of the liturgy in the baroque period, the effects of which continued to be felt throughout the romantic period and beyond. He pointed out the rise of a tendency to regard liturgy as purely ceremonial. Like court ceremonial, its purpose was to give honor and to impress those gathered with the grandeur of the place and the persons involved. Liturgical rites were "the etiquette of the great King" and they were expected to impress the grandeur of God and the church upon those who attended. The more obscure and rarified the gestures, the better. Baroque churches increasingly resembled theaters, and what the people watched was the ceremonial display. Bouyer devastatingly concluded that even nonbelievers come to church for its pomp at key moments of life, such as weddings, because ceremonies are regarded as what the church does best.[5]

All this was a far cry from the robust ecclesial sensibility that gave birth to the church's coherent liturgical tradition in the first place. As an action of the whole Body of Christ, head and members, the liturgy was never intended to be the province of clerics alone, or the backdrop for private devotions, or a ceremonial display for silent spectators. Yet it had become all these things.

As Romano Guardini once observed, the success of a renewed liturgy depends upon people reclaiming a "forgotten way of doing things."[6] In order for the church again to celebrate the liturgy with a sense of its true nature, it had to "remember" what liturgy was in the tradition that had slipped away. Clues to better understanding and practice were indeed embedded in the scriptures and the liturgical texts themselves, which the church had carefully preserved through the centuries. Evidence of a better sensibility that once reigned in the church could be discovered through historical study, especially in the writings of the church fathers. And, finally, adaptations to the needs of the present era could give living expression to the church's liturgical tradition here and now. The first task, however, was to awaken a desire in the church to learn—or re-learn—that tradition and the spirituality that went with it.

As with any changes that occur over long periods of time, the process that had led to a liturgy ossified and removed from the people was not so easy to see from close up. Most Catholics regarded the liturgy they knew as natural, normal, God-given, and inevitable. It took the prophetic vision and courage of a few to activate the church's desire to renew its own liturgy. These were the gifts of the liturgical movement.

2. The Liturgical Movement

Two stages can be discerned in the history of this movement. The first was born in a monastic setting, at the Benedictine abbey of Solesmes in France. It was to be found subsequently in those abbeys that carried on the tradition of Solesmes in Germany: Bueron, founded in 1863, and Maria Laach, re-founded in 1893.

Dom Prosper Guéranger, who re-founded Solesmes in 1833 as a specifically liturgical project, was a leading influence in the initial stage of the movement's development. Reacting against liturgical experimentation and the neo-Gallican rites composed in France after the revolution (rites he condemned as a product of Jansenism), he wanted to celebrate liturgy using a purely Roman model and looked to the medieval period to provide it. He took a deep interest in the revival of Gregorian chant, which he wanted to see become the music of the whole Roman Catholic Church. He also wrote a massive pastoral work about the liturgical year: *L'Année liturgique*. Although he completed only nine of the twelve planned volumes of this work, it had the effect of generating considerable interest in the liturgical year.

The German counterpart to the monastic renewal of liturgy in France took a somewhat different direction. It was very much influenced by the patristic revival at the University of Tübingen, and consequently reaped the benefits of a broader view of the history of the liturgy.[7] Since the patristic period was a time when many fundamental elements of the liturgy could be seen with great clarity, study of this period proved extremely useful in gaining insight into basic questions about the liturgy.

The problems and limitations of the first stage of the liturgical movement are generally acknowledged. Working with limited resources of scholarship, Guéranger's conclusions about liturgy were at times inaccurate and misleading. He was dismissive of the Eastern rites for example, and relied too heavily on medieval liturgical models that were themselves composites and hardly the "purest" form of liturgy. Furthermore, the lessons learned by application of liturgical principles to a monastic setting did not translate well into a parish environment. Finally, the desire to recreate an ideal liturgy of the past was deeply problematic. Many years later, it would be criticized by Pope Pius XII as "antiquarianism,"[8] and set aside as the movement settled into its deeper and truer course.

Nevertheless, Guéranger at Solesmes and the brothers Maurus and Placidus Wolther at Beuron and Maria Laach made a significant contribution. Their efforts succeeded in putting liturgy at the forefront of questions concerning church renewal. When Pope Pius X in 1903 issued his motu proprio on sacred music, *Tra le Sollecitudini*, the influence of the liturgical movement was everywhere evident in it. In fact, it is doubtful the document would ever have been written had it not been for the movement begun at these French and German monasteries. This motu proprio enunciated for the first time the concept that was to power the liturgical reform movement for the entire ensuing century: "...Our people assemble for the purpose of acquiring the true Christian spirit from its first and indispensable source, namely, active participation in the most sacred mysteries and in the public and solemn prayer of the Church."[9] The conviction that "active participation" in the liturgy is the "indispensable source" of the "true Christian spirit" became the heart and soul of the liturgical movement of the twentieth century.

One can trace a kind of monastic "family line" from the first stage of the movement to the second, which begins in 1909 and is often considered the movement proper. The Abbey of Maredsous in Belgium was founded in 1872 by Maurus Wolther, then abbot of Beuron. This abbey continued the work of making accessible the liturgical tradition of the church. It was known for its publication of the first Latin-French missal in 1882, and in 1884 it began publishing a periodical called *Messager des Fidèles* (called *Revue Bénédictine* from 1890 onwards) to support the liturgical movement. In 1899, the abbey of Mont César in Louvain was in turn founded by monks from Maredsous.

In 1906, a young diocesan priest who had served as a teacher and a labor chaplain in Liège was drawn to monastic life and entered the abbey at Mont César. His name was Lambert Beauduin. He became the catalyst for the development of a whole new phase of the liturgical movement. Through his passion for liturgy and church, his practical orientation, and his pastoral focus, Lambert Beauduin played a pivotal role in bringing the liturgical movement to ever-widening circles. In 1909, he delivered a paper on "The Prayer of the Church" at the National Congress on Catholic Works in Malines, and there met with a Catholic layman, Godefroid Kurth, to work out a plan of action that they would implement with the approval of the bishop of Brussels. This event marks the beginning of the phase that many historians regard as the liturgical movement proper.

At first, the movement was oriented not toward reform but simply toward education. It deepened its wisdom, broadened its knowledge base, and got more people involved in its work. The movement drew into its service brilliant pastoral thinkers, such as Odo Casel and Romano Guardini in Germany, Pius Parsch and Josef Jungmann in Austria, and Virgil Michel in the United States, to name only a few. Scholarship in liturgical studies increased. Numerous publications on the liturgy were produced and widely disseminated. Study seminars, known as "Liturgical Weeks," were organized for priests and pastors to improve their knowledge and understanding of liturgical issues. Translations of liturgical texts appeared for parish use. Liturgical institutes sprang up to provide education for future seminary teachers. The connection between liturgical renewal and social justice was explored, especially by Virgil Michel in the United States.[10]

As time went on, the efforts of the movement focused increasingly on bringing the liturgy to the people. No longer was it primarily monastic in inspiration and outlook. It became pastoral. It also became reformist. The fruit of scholarship and teaching was building a consensus that certain changes to the liturgy could bring about great benefit for the faithful. Liturgical studies had shown the possibility of more authentic expressions of the church's liturgical tradition, which was being hindered by the status quo. With the growth in knowledge and understanding, more people became eager to achieve reform.

As the movement gained momentum and became worldwide, it did so against a background of entrenched resistance to change. The liturgy was presumed to be unchanging and unchangeable. After the reforms of Pope Pius X near the turn of the century,[11] the impetus "from above" fizzled, and new initiatives hardly found an enthusiastic reception in Rome. It is therefore even more remarkable that the movement continued to grow. Experiments were tried with the vernacular, with Mass facing the people, and with the "Missa recitata" or "dialogue Mass" in which the people said the responses formerly offered only by the acolytes. Then, during the pontificate of Pope Pius XII, the door began to open a bit further for liturgical reform at higher levels in the church. This in turn sparked new efforts on the ground. More permissions were sought and obtained to try new things. Greater use of the vernacular in the liturgy was introduced on an experimental basis and met with great success. Evening Masses were tried. The eucharistic fast for communion at such Masses was reduced. Attempts were made at the restoration of the adult catechumenate, particularly in mission territories. All of these things were attempted as experiments long before any changes were legislated in the church at large. Gradually, the liturgical movement spread worldwide. As the pastoral direction of the work developed, the sentiment in favor of a general reform of the liturgy grew.

3. The Reforms of Pope Pius XII

In the midst of this ferment of interest in liturgical renewal, Pope Pius XII proved to be a decisive actor. When Pope Pius XII wrote his encyclical, *Mediator Dei*, in 1947, he gave the stamp of papal approval to the liturgical movement and heightened the prestige of its work. He explicitly commended those involved and fully embraced the principle of internal and external participation in the liturgy, which had been the goal of so much work up to this time. He stated in no uncertain terms that "all the faithful should be aware that to participate in the eucharistic sacrifice is their chief duty and supreme dignity, and that not in an inert and negligent fashion" but rather with "earnestness and concentration."[12] He urged that the people offer themselves, united to the sacrifice of Christ—a concept that would return at Vatican II—and quoted Pope Innocent III in support of the idea that the faithful offer the sacrifice along with the priest.[13]

Pope Pius XII also linked the efforts of the liturgical movement to his own decision, in 1945, to authorize a new translation of the psalms. Indeed, renewal in the area of biblical studies walked hand in hand with liturgical reform. So did ecumenism. Pope Pius XII's deep interest in reunion with the Orthodox is one of the outstanding features of his pontificate. His acknowledgment in *Mystici Corporis* (1943) of those who are united to the Body of Christ "by some unconscious yearning or desire" also opened the way to ecumenism. (Many of the leaders of the liturgical movement were also deeply involved with ecumenism. Lambert Beauduin even founded a monastic community dedicated to this endeavor.) This trio of encyclicals from Pope Pius XII—*Mediator Dei* (on the liturgy), *Divino Afflante Spiritu* (permitting the use of modern scripture scholarship), and *Mystici Corporis* (on the Mystical Body of Christ)—together had a tremendous influence on renewal movements at the time.

The pope's endorsement of liturgical renewal was not a blank check. He reproved those who took initiatives without permission. He chastised the over-zealous. He frowned on those who would do away with private Masses or statues or black vestments or devotions to the Sacred Heart. He praised Latin.

At the same time, however, he warned those who were apathetic or opposed to liturgical renewal that they should take no comfort from his words. While he affirmed the idea of objective reality in worship, he criticized partisans of an "objective piety" who sought to minimize subjective engagement in the liturgical action. He warmly approved of a "return to the sources"—the study of liturgical history—even though he condemned antiquarianism. He blasted those who claim Mass is invalid when only the priest takes communion, but he reprimanded any priest who would deny communion to the faithful during Mass itself. He also praised the faithful who desire to receive hosts consecrated at the Mass they attend rather than from the reserved sacrament in the tabernacle. In support of this, he cited Pope Benedict XIV—hardly a wild-eyed radical—writing in 1741.[14]

He became positively lyrical when describing the pastoral care of the church for the faithful, exercised through its liturgical rites:

> Let all, then, who would live in Christ flock to their priests. By them they will be supplied with the comforts and food of the spiritual life. From them they will procure the medicine of salvation assuring their cure and happy recovery from the fatal sickness of their sins. The priest, finally, will bless their homes, consecrate their families and help them, as they breathe their last, across the threshold of eternal happiness.[15]

He likewise gave a beautiful overview of the liturgical year, from a pastoral perspective, calling the whole church to meditate on the mysteries of Christ's life and imitate them through the cycle of the year.

The encyclical *Mediator Dei* was only one of the contributions of an official nature that Pope Pius XII made to liturgical reform. As early as 1946, he asked the Congregation of Rites to study the possibility of a complete reform of the liturgy. He also established a commission for liturgical reform, which functioned from 1948 to 1960. This commission was composed completely of scholars. Some of the people on it didn't know quite what they were supposed to be doing, but the body nevertheless accomplished some amazing things. Its work—carried on completely in secrecy—was closely monitored by Pope Pius XII, even during his illness, through reports from Monsignor Giovanni Battista Montini, director of internal affairs, and Father Augustin Bea, who was the pope's confessor and had weekly access to him.[16] Bea, who would later play an important role at Vatican II and become the first head of the Secretariat for Promoting Christian Unity, was appointed to the commission by Pope Pius XII and served on it continuously. Montini, of course, was later to become Pope Paul VI and shepherd the reforms initiated at the council to their completion.

By the end of its existence, the Pian commission had revised all the liturgical books. Not all were published however, because by the time they were finished the Second Vatican Council was already looming. Two specific accomplishments of this body during the pontificate of Pope Pius XII stand out, however: the reform of the Easter Vigil in 1951 and the reform of the rest of Holy Week in 1955. Less widely acclaimed, but also significant, was the simplification of the rubrics that Pope Pius XII decreed in 1955.

Many Catholics today are accustomed to thinking that the liturgical reforms of recent history began with Vatican II. While it is true that Vatican II inaugurated the most thoroughgoing liturgical reform of modern times, including a review and further revision of these works of the 1950s, the efforts of the Pian commission before Vatican II did result in official reforms of some consequence and should not be overlooked. They paved the way for acceptance of liturgical reform itself and encouraged expectations of its success. At the same time, the changes they produced were somewhat nonthreatening in that they left untouched the major concern of all parties: the Mass itself.

The Easter Vigil provides a good illustration of the Pian reform. If ever there was an ossified and neglected treasure of the liturgical tradition, the Easter Vigil was it. The oldest—and originally the church's only—celebration of Easter, this splendid liturgy marking the paschal mystery had gone through a gradual decline, making it all but inaccessible to the faithful. Originally a night service, it had migrated to the early morning hours, even though the prayers continued to speak of "this night." Originally the starting point of the whole Easter season, it became so incoherent that it was followed by Lenten Vespers. Originally required of the faithful, attendance became optional and finally lapsed altogether in most places, leaving it to be "gotten out of the way" by the priest and a few altar boys on Holy Saturday morning. When Pope Pius XII reformed this liturgy, not too many of the faithful even knew what it was.

A great deal of sophistication went into making the reform of the Easter Vigil both pastoral and reflective of a rich and varied liturgical tradition.[17] Some of the prayers that represented unnecessary duplications, built up over the centuries, were removed. Certain puzzling elements of the 1570 ritual, such as the carrying of three candles on a spear-shaped rod, were replaced with more effective symbols. Although care was taken to honor distinctively Roman aspects of the Vigil, contributions were welcomed from other sources, such as the Mozarabic rite, which had been limited historically by imposition of the Roman rite in the West. Sources from the East, such as the Jerusalem liturgy, were consulted. No one historical period was used exclusively as the model. New texts were also written and included. For example, the liturgy contained a renewal of baptismal promises by the assembly—something never before seen in the liturgy.[18] Most revolutionary of all, participation of the people was written into the rubrics for the first time,[19] and pastors were enjoined to encourage their people to participate.

The results were stunning. First of all, people came. They had many things to do in the liturgy and the liturgy itself was coherent and affecting. The lighting of the new fire took place at night, emphasizing the contrast between darkness and light. A candle ceremony derived from the liturgy in Jerusalem allowed all the faithful to participate in the service of light with candles of their own. The number of Old Testament readings was reduced, making it easier for the people to remain attentive. The turning point of the celebration was at the numinous hour of midnight, when the Eucharist began and the Vigil turned into Easter day. The Vigil once again inaugurated the Easter feast, as it had done originally. Annibale Bugnini, secretary to the Pian commission, called the response that greeted the reform of the Easter Vigil in 1951 "an explosion of joy."[20]

At the same time, seen within its full context, the reform was a fairly modest step. Those who did not welcome change could go to Mass on Easter Sunday and find everything the same as it always had been.

The first International Congress of Pastoral Liturgy was held in Assisi in 1956. This congress was very important to the convergence of interest and support for liturgical renewal that found expression in the council. Jungmann's talk "The Pastoral Idea in the History of the Liturgy" and Bea's "The Pastoral Value of the Word of God in the Sacred Liturgy" were especially influential. Pope Pius XII said in the opening of his own address that "The liturgical movement is . . . a sign of the providential dispositions of God in the present time [and] of the movement of the Holy Spirit in the Church."[21]

Pope John XXIII continued the progress begun under his predecessor. It was he who authorized the publication of the new Breviary and

Pontifical in 1962. But it was, of course, the Second Vatican Council that would take up the cause of liturgical reform and renewal in an all-embracing way.

So we see that the situation on the eve of the council was in many respects ripe for the production of serious and important work on the liturgy. The idea of liturgical renewal had an international base in a movement that had been growing for more than half a century. It had enjoyed the support of three popes, each in his own way. The people working on this project at all levels had established a reputation for pastoral concern. And, finally, the kind of research undertaken in advance of the reform was reasonably mature and had a creditable claim to both religious and scholarly integrity.

THE CONSTITUTION ON THE SACRED LITURGY TAKES SHAPE

When Pope John XXIII called a council in 1962, a preparatory commission was established to work on the liturgy. This commission was a much larger and more diverse body than the Pian commission had been, numbering more than ninety people. It was comprised of pastors as well as scholars from a variety of disciplines, and they were drawn from twenty-five nations. As Bugnini was careful to note in his account of the process, one could easily have recruited this many nationalities from among people living in Rome itself, but special effort was made to include people who actually lived and worshiped in different lands, including mission territories and communities under oppression.[22]

This body was divided into twelve subgroups to work on specific issues. A thirteenth was then added to address the general question of the relationship of liturgy to the life of the church. The section this last subgroup produced was placed first because of its overarching nature, and it became the most important of all. Together, the commission produced four successive drafts of a document that would later be submitted to the council.

Two topics proved contentious during this phase of the process: sacred music and the use of Latin. The person assigned to head the committee on sacred music, Monsignor Igino Anglés Pamiés of Spain, dean of the Pontifical Institute of Sacred Music in Rome, would not work with the others appointed, and maligned the motives of the commission to outsiders. He claimed—among other things—that this body was the "number one enemy of Latin," which was not true.[23] Behind the assault was firm opposition to congregational singing, which, it was feared, would displace the role of the choir and destroy the patrimony of sacred music treasured by the church in recent centuries.

Here one begins to see opposition coalescing and at times taking a nasty turn, because actual widespread changes were finally about to happen. The liturgical movement had set the agenda up to this point, moving against the backdrop of entrenched practices that many thought never could or would change. There was no "counter–liturgical movement" during the first half of the twentieth century. But as the principles of liturgical renewal—particularly the principle of active participation—were now poised to "take the field" and be incorporated into the official teaching and discipline of the church, opposition arose and became more vocal.

The same kind of resistance arose in connection with the discussion of Latin. The possibility of using the vernacular in liturgy raised deep anxieties and became a rallying point of opposition to all liturgical reform.

The preparatory commission, interestingly enough, was made up of people who held a wide variety of positions on the question, and in sum had no intention of discontinuing the use of Latin. It proposed that priests continue to be trained in Latin and conduct their own prayer exclusively in Latin, and the vernacular be used in liturgies with the people only when this was deemed helpful for pastoral reasons. But *any* use of the vernacular awakened a panic in certain church circles—Latin is being taken away! The language of the liturgy emerged as a flashpoint for conflict.

There was a subgroup devoted to the subject of Latin, but the document it produced was deemed too confusing.[24] The secretariat for the commission saw a storm brewing, and for the sake of prudence wanted not to deal with the subject as a separate item on the agenda of a plenary meeting but rather to have it addressed under various headings. The proponents of Latin, however, wanted a general debate, and the president of the commission, Cardinal Gaetano Cicognani, permitted it, adding his own voice to the discussion. The results were very moving, as both sides presented their points of view. The final outcome can be seen in chapter 1 of the constitution, which speaks to values on both sides of the question.

After all the editing of the drafts had been completed, Cardinal Cicognani as president was presented with a text of the full document for his signature. He signed it on February 1, 1962, and died four days later.

Cicognani was replaced by the new prefect of the Congregation of Rites, Cardinal Arcadio M. Larraona, CMF, on February 22. This was the same day Pope John XXIII promulgated an apostolic constitution aimed at strengthening the study of Latin. Cardinal Larraona did not look kindly on the document that had just been signed by Cicognani. He regarded it as too "progressive." So he gathered a secret committee to rewrite it—removing measures such as communion under both forms for the laity and decentralization of decision-making. The new document restricted concelebration and the use of the vernacular, and it limited the scope of the document, reserving all practical decisions to the pope. It also removed the notes that had been attached to the original, explaining the background of each article. This new text was then sent through the required approval process external to the commission and was quickly distributed to the council fathers as the text approved by the coordinating committee.

The switch between the document actually produced by the preparatory commission and the one manufactured by the "ghost commission" assembled by Larraona was, needless to say, discovered. Those who had worked on the preparatory commission shared the information that was lacking in the text the fathers received. The material that had been deleted was re-introduced. The final outcome was that the original measures were passed—ultimately with very few changes—despite this attempt to water down the text.

The outcome was a setback for the opposition. It was accompanied by another blow of a more personal and tragic sort. The secret rewriting of the document had been entrusted to a Father Joseph Löw, CSSR, a brilliant Redemptorist who had worked on the Pian commission. Löw died unexpectedly on September 23, and it took some time for the opposition to regroup. In the meantime, the council had moved forward.

The work of the preparatory commission was, on the whole, well received by the council fathers. The document was well-written, meticulously researched, and mercifully short. Revisions were suggested by the council fathers. A conciliar commission was assembled to incorporate these revisions into the document. They did so with the help of twenty-six experts who were put in service to the project initially, and more who were appointed later. All of this took place with great dispatch.

Liturgy was placed first on the agenda of the council in 1962, and its placement up front was to signal the pastoral dimension of the entire council. The discussion also became a proving ground for how to conduct the business of the council. From October 22 to November 14, 1962, the council fathers discussed the proposed document that was to become the Constitution on the Sacred Liturgy. Fifteen sessions were devoted to this discussion.

There were fifty hours of debate, 387 oral interventions, and 297 interventions submitted in writing. Although many topics were discussed, debates on the floor were most heated, not surprisingly, when it came to Latin. There were 80 interventions on the subject of language alone. Some of the most vocal opposition to change came from Americans. In the discussion of the vernacular, Cardinal James Francis McIntyre of Los Angeles stated flatly that "The Sacred Mass should remain as it is. Serious changes in liturgy introduce serious changes in dogma."[25] Cardinal Francis Spellman of New York protested vigorously against the document's provision for inculturation (article 37).[26] Along with the leader of the conservative opposition from the Roman Curia, Cardinal Alfredo Ottaviani, Spellman painted a dire picture of what ills would befall the church if this and other of the reforms were to take place.[27] Ironically, it was two American priests on the preparatory commission who had argued most convincingly for the vernacular: Dom Godfrey Diekmann of Saint John's Abbey in Collegeville and Father Frederick MacManus of Catholic University in Washington.[28]

Scholarship on the question of Latin in the liturgy was clear: there is no basis for arguing that Latin is divinely sanctioned or intended by God as the sole and eternal tongue of the liturgy. Examples of ancient liturgies in other languages abound and have an unarguable claim to authenticity. The church did not set out to create a separate "sacral" language for its worship. Latin was adopted in the West as a *living* language for the liturgy. It lost that role historically when the Romance and Germanic languages usurped its place as the living languages of those cultures. During the Reformation however, the Catholic Church repudiated use of the vernacular because it was championed by the reformers. Translation of liturgical texts at that time could not be guaranteed safe from theological confusion and errors precisely because it was a time of great turmoil. But this had nothing to do with what languages Pilate's inscription on the cross were written in, or claims of unalterable tradition, or any of the other spurious arguments usually presented.[29]

When the debate on the liturgy constitution had finished in November 1962, no one knew how the voting would go. Much time, after all, had been spent airing objections to the document. It was therefore an undisguised triumph when the document was approved on November 14, 1962, by a vote of 2,162 in favor and 46 opposed (with 7 ballots declared void). All the negative comments were emanating from only a little more than 2 percent of the council. This vote approved the "guiding norms" of the liturgy schema and pushed the document forward to the final stage of refinement that would result in the definitive text.

Pope John XXIII would not live to see the process come to completion. He died on June 3, 1963, and Cardinal Giovanni Battista Montini, Pope Paul VI, was elected his successor on June 21. Eighty-six amendments to the liturgy document were voted on in the course of twenty-two general meetings. After further revisions, final approval by the council fathers was given on December 4, 1963, in a vote of 2,147 for and 4 against.

The vote was announced in the full assembly of the council and in the presence of Pope Paul VI. Applause rose and echoed through the basilica. The applause resounded on and on—expressing sober yet heartfelt support for this effort and all it symbolized. The date was December 4, 1963: four hundred years to the day since the Council of Trent had decided to leave the question of liturgical reform to the Holy See, which then produced the Tridentine reform. Pope Paul VI, in promulgating the liturgy document, praised what the fathers had done in producing this first fruit of the council in these words:

> We may see in this an acknowledgement of a right order of values and duties: God in the first place; prayer our first duty; the liturgy the first school of spirituality, the first gift we can bestow on Christians who believe and pray with us. It is the

first invitation to the world to break forth in happy and truthful prayer and to feel the ineffable lifegiving force that comes from joining us in the song of divine praise and human hope, through Christ our Lord and in the Holy Spirit.[30]

The Constitution on the Sacred Liturgy stands at the head of all the work of the council—not only chronologically, but also as sign and symbol of the values and priorities of that council.

In the next chapter we will see what that document—approved so overwhelmingly—actually had to say.

PART II

MAJOR POINTS

Unlike the other documents of Vatican II, the Constitution on the Sacred Liturgy begins with a short introduction that situates the liturgy document within the aims of the council. This introduction concisely restates what Pope John XXIII had expressed as his own intentions for the council on several occasions. The first of these was on January 25, 1959, less than ninety days after his election to the papacy, when he announced to a small group of cardinals gathered at St. Paul's Outside the Walls that he would call both a Roman synod and a general church council and revise the code of canon law.

At that time, he described the council's aims as: "the enlightenment, edification, and joy of the entire Christian people" and "a renewed cordial invitation to the faithful of the separated churches to participate with us in this feast of grace and brotherhood, for which so many souls long in all parts of the world."[1] These gracious sentiments found their way into the opening of the Constitution on the Sacred Liturgy.

The placement of this list of aims at the head of *Sacrosanctum Concilium* is intended to show that the decision to reform the liturgy is closely allied with the purposes of the council itself. The aims of the council are:

– renewal of God's people

– adaptation to the times

– ecumenism, and

– evangelization

The next paragraph of the preface goes on to say that reform of the liturgy is critical to this agenda, because in the liturgy the church experiences and shows forth its true identity. The liturgy enables the church to pursue these four goals because it strengthens the faithful to go forth into today's world and carry on the mission of Christ and the Holy Spirit. The grace of God given to them through the liturgy enables them to be credible ambassadors of reconciliation among other Christians and effective evangelists among nonbelievers.

What is especially striking about these aims of the council is that they are so outward-directed. They describe an agenda that goes far beyond a simple attempt of the church to put its own house in order, codifying or correcting itself. The renewal of Christian liturgy was to be undertaken in light of the understanding that the church's ultimate goal is to reach beyond itself.

The introduction avoids a combative or condemnatory stance toward the outside world. This too is striking. The council could easily have taken a posture of disapproval and opposition to contemporary currents. This era in history included the rise of atheistic communism, gradual dechristianization of historically Christian nations, the arms race, and third-world wars of independence that were changing the political order. Indeed, in preparation for the council, a number of bishops from around the world submitted lists of what they wanted the council to condemn—perceived enemies, both without and within, such as communism, existentialism, the "new theology," and modernism.[2] Such calls were not permitted to shape the agenda of the council.

Instead, the overall direction described here was profoundly life-affirming. Its goal was not to throw up a higher wall to guard the church from the tumult of the times, much less to condemn the movements of history in the midst of which the church found itself. Its stated purpose was rather to renew the church from within so as to allow it to flourish and bear more abundant fruit in the present. It was to foster movement toward genuine unity among all Christians, and to offer a loving and persuasive invitation to those outside its fold to come and be fed.

What a bold agenda! What a tremendous dream. It is perhaps not surprising that forty years after the council many aspects of that dream still await fulfillment. Yet even from the vantage point of the present day, knowing how many obstacles remain to realizing the hopes of the council, these four aims retain their freshness and the liveliness of their challenge. Perhaps it is because they breathe the spirit of the gospel itself—an invitation to life in abundance.

The aims can help us measure subsequent progress against the standard they set, to see to what extent the vision has indeed been realized.

We will return to these points when we consider and evaluate developments after the council.

After stating the aims of the council and establishing the link between liturgy and this agenda, the introduction announces that the document will contain principles for the promotion and reform of the liturgy, as well as practical norms. These norms will apply mainly to the Roman rite, although some of them, by their nature, will apply to the other rites within Catholicism as well.[3]

Finally, the introduction affirms the value and dignity of all the lawfully established rites within the Catholic Church. This statement is of great importance to Eastern rite Catholics, who have at times been subjected to pressure to conform to the Roman rite at the expense of their own tradition. The statement was also carefully worded so that it could apply not only to rites currently part of the Catholic Church, but also to any that might come into communion with Rome in the future. Again, an outward-directed and ecumenical agenda can be seen at work here. Finally, the introduction, while affirming the dignity of "lawfully established" rites, does not exempt them from renewal. They too must be revised where necessary to meet the needs of modern times.[4]

This brief introduction leads into the seven chapters of the constitution. They cover in detail the nature and importance of the liturgy, norms for the reform of the liturgy in all its aspects, and the promotion of education and action in relation to the liturgy on parish and diocesan levels.

A great deal could be said about each article of the constitution. Rather than trying to summarize or comment on all the individual items however, we will focus on seven essential concepts in the document. They do not correspond to the chapter divisions, but are important to understanding the content of the document as a whole. The first five of these concepts, as I have organized them, provide a vision and understanding of the liturgy itself. They are the paschal mystery, liturgy as summit and source of the church's life, active participation, ecclesiology, and inculturation. The other two are practical corollaries that must be addressed if the paradigm or vision is to be realized. If the first five are the "what" of a renewed liturgy, the final two are the "how." They are the renewal of the liturgical books, music, art, and artifacts of the liturgy, and the education and formation of both the clergy and the faithful in liturgical matters.

Outline of *Sacrosanctum Concilium*

When considering the seven essential concepts discussed here, it is helpful to have a copy of the Constitution on the Sacred Liturgy on hand in order to see how they appear in the text itself. The document is organized as follows:

Introduction (articles 1–4)

Chapter I: General Principles for the Restoration and Promotion of the Sacred Liturgy

1. The Nature of the Sacred Liturgy and Its Importance in the Church's Life (articles 5–13)

2. The Promotion of Liturgical Instruction and Active Participation (articles 14–20)

3. The Reform of the Sacred Liturgy (articles 21–46)
   A. *General norms (22–25)*
   B. *Norms drawn from the hierarchic and communal nature of the Liturgy (26–32)*
   C. *Norms based upon the didactic and pastoral nature of the Liturgy (33–36)*
   D. *Norms for adapting the Liturgy to the culture and traditions of peoples (37–40)*
   E. *Promotion of Liturgical Life in Diocese and Parish (41–42)*
   F. *The Promotion of Pastoral-Liturgical Action (43–46)*

Chapter II: The Most Sacred Mystery of the Eucharist (articles 47–58)

Chapter III: The Other Sacraments and Sacramentals (articles 59–82)

Chapter IV: The Divine Office (articles 83–101)

Chapter V: The Liturgical Year (articles 102–111)

Chapter VI: Sacred Music (articles 112–121)

Chapter VII: Sacred Art and Sacred Furnishings (articles 122–130)

Appendix: A Declaration of the Second Ecumenical Council of the Vatican on Revision of the Calendar

SEVEN ESSENTIAL CONCEPTS

1. The Paschal Mystery

The paschal mystery is without a doubt the central theological concept of the liturgical renewal advanced at Vatican II. It appears ten times in the constitution itself and is repeated often in papal documents and official texts following the council. Subsequent papal documents, church pronouncements and instructions regarding the liturgy, and the *Catechism of the Catholic Church* would later use the expression frequently. It is the interpretive key that unlocks the meaning of the whole reform.

Although the term "paschal mystery" dates from the patristic period, it gained new prominence in liturgical discussions during the first half of the twentieth century. Dom Odo Casel, a monk of the Abbey of Maria Laach and pioneer of the liturgical movement, wrote extensively about the idea of the Christian mystery.[5] He began from the vantage point of liturgical history, theorizing that Christian liturgy owed something of its inspiration to the mystery cults of surrounding religions at the dawn of the Christian era. But his thinking went beyond a discussion of the history of religions to the recovery of an insight contained in the original Greek word *mysterion* of which the Latin word *sacramentum* is a translation. He seized on the idea of mystery as key to how human participation in the liturgy works, even now. The theology he developed was a way to answer the question of how the redemption won by Christ at a particular moment in history could become available to people in every historical epoch.[6] Casel's approach was not so much to ask how the mystery gets to us, but how we get to it. The liturgy, he argued, is how we enter the mystery.

By their exploration of the liturgical thinking of the patristic period, Casel and the school of Maria Laach also brought into currency the idea that the pre-eminent mystery that Christians enter through the liturgy is no less than the whole of Christ's death, resurrection, and glorification—in other words, the paschal mystery. The concept of the paschal mystery—without neglecting the saving passion—brings Christ's resurrection and glorification into full view. They are integral to the mystery of salvation.

While the church has always taught the resurrection as a truth of the faith, Catholics prior to Vatican II were accustomed to thinking exclusively of Christ's death on the cross as the saving event celebrated in the liturgy. When the resurrection was included in the document, therefore, some of the fathers at the council protested at first. Misunderstandings were dispelled, however, when references from the Roman Missal were incorporated into the text. These showed the legitimacy of the approach from the content of the church's liturgical prayer itself, and the idea was embraced.[7]

It must be stressed that the paschal mystery is not some sort of new concept, but indeed a very old one. Patristic texts and ancient liturgies give ample evidence of such thinking, and indeed are impossible to interpret if one does not understand the integration of liturgy, theology, and Christian life that is presumed by the idea of mystery.

It is important to note that "mystery" in this theological sense is not something that disappears upon investigation, as does a mystery that is solved in a crime novel. Neither is mystery something to which the door of knowledge is firmly closed, like a statement that defies all rational argument and must therefore be taken on faith. A mystery in the theological sense implied by the term "paschal mystery" is rather a truth so deep you cannot see the end of it. A mystery is something you can explore without ever exhausting its treasures. It is in the nature of a mystery such as this that God invites people into it and the church guides them around in it, as in a city.[8] The faithful are endlessly discovering the richness of such a mystery. Without defining or limiting it, human understanding, like sonar, plumbs its depths.[9]

Looking back on the rise to prominence of the concept of the paschal mystery as a way of talking about liturgy, one can see the great attractiveness of it from a variety of standpoints. The paschal mystery was a profoundly counter-cultural way to describe the essence of Christianity in the modern era. In an age of rationalism and materialism, to speak of mystery is nonsense—or Christian sense, depending on your point of view. Although not incompatible with scholastic theology, the idea of mystery also went beyond the dry and stale dissections typical of textbook sacramental theology before the council. It was fresh and new. By exploring the idea of the paschal mystery, Western Christians were also beginning to speak a language that could better relate to the East, and this served ecumenism. Finally, the idea of mystery held a kind of popular appeal as well, because it assumed an attitude of humility before matters that go beyond our power to fully comprehend.

The concept of the paschal mystery points to an inner dynamism at the heart of the liturgy itself. If what we enter into in the liturgy is Christ's passover from death to life, we participate in a transforming event. The paschal mystery keeps us mindful of the cost of discipleship, yet confident of the "city yet to come, which we seek" (*SC*, 2). Through the idea of the paschal mystery, the masterful synthesis of Augustine concerning the meaning of the pascha—that in Christ's "passing over" from this world to the Father humanity too "passes over" from the old life of sin to the new life of grace[10]—emerged like a golden thread running through the whole liturgical life of the church. The focus of the preceding era, which had been on human guilt for sin and its expiation through the sacrifice of Christ, the sinless Victim, at the hands of the priest, was radically changed by the ascendance of the concept of the paschal mystery. The cross was not, as it were, the end of the story, but its ever-renewed beginning.

The theory that Christians borrowed liturgical elements from mystery religions of the first century has of course been debated and critiqued by subsequent historical study, but the council left aside all such controversies. The concept of the paschal mystery was used simply as a way to describe the saving work of Christ, and our participation in it through the liturgy.

2. Liturgy as "Summit and Source" of the Church's Life

The place of the liturgy in the life of the church was a topic of great interest to those who wrote the constitution. A correct understanding of the relationship between liturgy and church was not something that could be taken for granted; it needed to be stated.

The essential concept that emerged in the document and has since been quoted repeatedly in the decades following the council is found in article 10: "[T]he liturgy is the summit toward which the activity of the Church is directed...it is the font from which all her power flows."

There were a number of objections to this idea raised in discussion at the council. Some of the fathers were uncomfortable with assigning such a central role to the liturgy. The purpose of the church is to save souls and glorify God; the liturgy is a means to an end, not a goal in itself, they argued. The source of the church's life is Jesus Christ and the Holy Spirit, not the liturgy. Upon thorough discussion, however, these misgivings were put to rest. It was clarified that the very reason for the liturgy being the summit and source is the action of Christ and the Holy Spirit within it, sanctifying humans and giving glory to God. In the end, the statement was passed unchanged, by a strong majority vote.

The constitution is careful to point out that the church must do other things in addition to the liturgy. Preaching, evangelization, and conversion must pave the way to participation in the sacraments and the prayer of the church. But the purpose of all the activity that leads people to worship is the act of worship itself. The efforts of the church are expended tirelessly outside the liturgy precisely so that people can stand together in faithful worship, in the midst of a believing community, and share in the sacrifice and banquet of the Eucharist.

There is a point here not to be missed. Liturgy is not merely instrumental. It helps, strengthens, and enables God's people to further the mission of Christ and to hasten the coming of the kingdom, and as such is an instrument of sanctification. In this sense it is the means to an end. But a purely pragmatic or functional analysis of liturgy leads astray those who would understand its meaning. Liturgy is "a foretaste of the heavenly liturgy" (*SC*, 8), a sharing in the transcendent mystery of God in Christ and of Christ in the church. It is the perfect praise of the Eternal Father in the Spirit by the Son, and thus the "summit." The high point of our life of faith is the liturgy—not understood as a particular form of words or collection of rubrics, but as graced participation in the worship of God by those who have been won for him in Christ.

The idea of the liturgy as "summit and source" is based on the notion that the liturgy is the priestly action of Jesus Christ and of his Body, the church. It is Christ himself who acts in the liturgy. The faithful are joined to Christ in the "great work" of glorifying God and sanctifying humanity through the liturgy (*SC*, 7), and for this reason it is the most exalted activity we undertake. Borrowing from Pope Pius XI's encyclical *Divini Cultus* (1929), the constitution makes it clear that nothing is more important: "[E]very liturgical celebration, because it is an action of Christ the priest and of His Body which is the Church, is a sacred action surpassing all others; no other action of the Church can equal its efficacy by the same title and to the same degree" (*SC*, 7).

In explaining the liturgy as the action of Christ himself, the constitution goes on to enumerate several ways that Christ is present in the liturgy:

- Christ is present in the person of the minister.
- Christ is especially present under the eucharistic species.
- Christ is present in the celebration of the sacraments.
- Christ is present in his Word, proclaimed in the liturgy.
- Christ is present when the assembly prays and sings.

This enumeration of the presences of Christ may not seem very remarkable. For the most part they are identical to those outlined by Pope Pius XII in *Mediator Dei* (*MD*, 20). There the pope listed Christ's presence in the minister, the sacraments, and the eucharistic species in almost exactly these same words. Even the idea of Christ present in the assembly when its members pray and sing is found in *Mediator Dei*, and indeed, is founded on the scriptures themselves (Matt 18:20).

There is one item here, however, that stands out as new: Christ's presence in his Word. This explicit recognition of Christ's presence in the Word was made to advance an ecumenical spirit.[11] Indeed, the practical implications of this acknowledgment would go a long way toward improving the climate for dialogue with churches descended from the Reformation in the West. Within the Catholic community itself during the two decades prior to the council, renewed attention had been given to the study of sacred scripture, encouraged by Pope Pius XII's encyclical, *Divino Afflante Spiritu* (1943). Also, under Pope Pius XII, Catholics had been participating in the ecumenical movement since the 1940s (and unofficially before that time). The recognition of Christ's presence in the Word thus forged a link between these developments and the liturgical reform. The constitution later points out that it is "essential" to the success of the liturgical reform for the church to cultivate a "warm and living love for scripture" (*SC*, 24). In the liturgy, the constitution asserted, "Christ is still proclaiming His gospel" (*SC*, 33). The affirmation of Christ's presence in the Word was therefore an important—and new—aspect of the Catholic Church's recognition of the importance of scripture in its life as a whole. The identification of the scriptures with

Christ is of course quite old,[12] but affirming the presence of Christ in the Word in the liturgy was a fresh and striking addition.

If the liturgy is summit and source, other matters must necessarily be ordered to it. In the experience of many people over the preceding centuries, devotions had completely eclipsed the liturgy as the principal nourishment of the spiritual life, and the sanctoral calendar easily over-shadowed the seasons of the liturgical year. By affirming the centrality of the liturgy, the constitution was saying all this had to change.

The Constitution on the Sacred Liturgy echoes Pope Pius XII, but it also goes a step beyond him. In *Mediator Dei*, although Pope Pius XII had encouraged the faithful to participate in the liturgy, he waved away the idea that everybody could do so. His assumption was that some people are incapable of such participation and should be left to their devotions, which are good enough (*MD*, 103).

When the constitution speaks of devotions, it does so with warmth and respect. Its final word, however, is this: "But these devotions should be so drawn up that they harmonize with the liturgical seasons, accord with the sacred liturgy, are in some fashion derived from it, and lead the people to it, since, in fact, the liturgy by its very nature far surpasses any of them" (*SC*, 13). Of the celebrations of the saints, the constitution recommends that many of these be kept selectively by local communities, "Lest the feasts of the saints should take precedence over the feasts which commemorate the very mysteries of salvation..." (*SC*, 111).

By calling liturgy the summit and source of the Christian life, the constitution asserted a strategic priority. It laid a foundation for the claim that the liturgical formation of clergy and liturgical catechesis of the faithful are not optional but essential. Although the liturgical movement had succeeded in establishing liturgical institutes in many countries, such institutions were few in number, and certainly had not influenced every seminary or house of religious studies. The study of liturgy was now slated to become a high priority item. The teaching of scripture and theology and all areas of religious studies would have to take liturgy into account.

The idea of the liturgy as "summit and source" also brought the liturgical action to the fore. The cult of the Eucharist was never mentioned in the constitution. What was deemed necessary, rather, was renewed attention to the *celebration* of the Eucharist as the summit and source of Christian life.

3. Full, Active, and Conscious Participation

No value is voiced with greater frequency in the constitution than the "full, active, and conscious participation" of the faithful. The concept of active participation arises at least fourteen times—more, if you count elements that are indissolubly linked to it, such as the instruction to provide rubrics for the people's part in the liturgy. Indeed, it appears in the document so often that one of the early commentators on the constitution compared it to the response to the litanies! Ever since Pope Pius X lauded active participation in 1903, it has been synonymous with the renewal sought by the liturgical movement. Lambert Beauduin and the leaders of the movement used it for many years before a council was even dreamed about. As we saw earlier, Pope Pius XII added his voice in support of the same principle when he wrote at length about the liturgy in *Mediator Dei*.

The expression is never defined in the document. Nevertheless, it would be wrong to see it as a mere slogan, devoid of concrete content. On the contrary, it contains a great wealth of meaning. The participation envisioned most certainly includes a complete sharing in all the words, music, gestures, and actions of the Mass that are proper to the people. Participation will at times include sharing of the chalice (*SC*, 55) and certainly extends to sharing in the elements consecrated at the Mass itself (*SC*, 55) in communion. Participation includes being nourished by the word of God (*SC*, 51), taking part in the prayer of the faithful (*SC*, 53), offering the sacrifice with the priest, and offering oneself as well (*SC*, 48). It may be fostered by the use of the vernacular in readings, prayers, and song (*SC*, 36, 54). Participation extends to "bodily attitudes" and to silence too (*SC*, 30).

The active participation envisioned also includes the inner or subjective dimension of participation that is spiritual, moral, and intellectual. It would never be enough simply to take proper postures, make the correct gestures, or mouth the words of prayers and songs. Twice the document says of participants in the liturgy that "their minds should be attuned to their voices"—once in discussing the overall dispositions required of the faithful who take part in the liturgy (*SC*, 11) and again in discussing the participation of both clergy and laity in the Divine Office (*SC*, 90).

The document also poignantly names what it wants by saying what it does *not* want. "The Church, therefore, earnestly desires that Christ's faithful, when present at this mystery of faith, should not be there as strangers or silent spectators..." (*SC*, 48). Rather, by participation in the liturgy, the people "...should be drawn day by day into ever more perfect union with God and with each other, so that finally God may be all in all."

"Full, active, and conscious participation" is the pearl of great price of the liturgical reform. Other less important values must be traded in order to secure it. For example, musical settings of the Mass that do not include an appropriate part for the people will no longer be regarded as suitable for worship (*SC*, 114, 141). The faithful must say goodbye to "Father's Mass" in which everything is done for them, because the priest celebrant will now perform this ritual in dialogue with the people whenever they are present (*SC*, 27). Finally, the concept of liturgical participation includes more than rearranging texts, changing rubrics, or moving furniture. It is a matter of conversion of heart, of saying an "amen" that makes a difference.

This mandate for participation would have a profound effect ultimately upon the work of catechesis. Historically, an overemphasis on God's all-sufficient action in the sacraments (*ex opere operato*) had reduced the perception that people need to be catechized in relation to the liturgy in order to experience its benefits. In response to the challenge of the Reformation, the Catholic Church had focused almost exclusively on the issue of sacramental efficacy and not upon the richness of the sacramental signs themselves. According to this mindset, the rites, correctly performed, delivered grace "automatically," as it were. The right "dispositions" for fruitful reception of the sacraments were gained through a piety quite removed from any actual engagement with the ritual itself. To toil at improving the quality of the celebration, or to expend effort in preparing people to celebrate or to reflect on the celebration afterwards, would not have occurred to anybody, given the assumptions they had. The Constitution on the Sacred Liturgy however, with its emphasis on active participation, fully approved—indeed necessitated—a plunge into waters of liturgical experience from the shores of an abstract concept of sacramental efficacy. It would require zealous pastors and catechists to teach people how to swim in these new waters. Indeed, numerous references to teaching exist in the document (see *SC*, 14–19, 35.3, 105, 115, etc.). The early work of the liturgical movement in this regard is likewise endorsed and promoted as exemplary: "Zeal for the promotion and restoration of the liturgy" is deemed "a movement of the Holy Spirit," and "a distinguishing mark of the Church's life..." (*SC*, 43).

4. Ecclesiology

Participation in the liturgy had been called the "right and duty" of the faithful by Pope Pius XII. But the constitution goes further to say that participation in the liturgy is their right and duty "by reason of their baptism" (*SC*, 14). The document recognizes baptismal dignity at the very outset of the discussion of liturgical promotion and participation. This theme was to emerge even more strongly in the post-conciliar era.

It is through baptism that the faithful "are plunged into the paschal mystery of Christ," which is the core of what the liturgy celebrates (*SC*, 6). The constitution proposes for baptism itself a thorough and far-reaching liturgical reform: restoration of the adult catechumenate received in stages (*SC*, 64), provision of both a solemn and a simple rite of adult baptism (*SC*, 66), reform of the rite of infant baptism (*SC*, 67), a new way to "supply the rites" that are lacking when someone is baptized in danger of death and to receive baptized Christians into the full communion of the Catholic Church (*SC*, 69), and a recognition of lay administration of baptism in exceptional cases (*SC*, 68). The priesthood of the baptized, although different in nature from the ministerial priesthood, is respected (*SC*, 48, 53).

The liturgical reform did not raise the profile of the baptized at the expense of the ordained. What surfaced was a rather modest recognition of the dignity of baptism, bringing the ensemble of orders within the church into better balance. The ministerial priesthood retained prominence, but the role of the people in the liturgy began to be on the radar scope, at long last. Thus, the constitution proposed a return to a more traditional—that is, higher—value placed on baptism.

The dignity of the baptismal priesthood comes to light in a special way in article 48, which speaks of the people offering the sacrifice "with" the priest. Father Josef Jungmann, SJ, a peritus at the council, observed of article 48: "Without using the word 'common priesthood,' this was in fact what was stressed here with the greatest vigor."[13] At the time, it was considered an outstanding concession.

Beyond addressing the general role of the liturgical assembly, the constitution established the fact that certain liturgical ministries are properly exercised by laypeople. They are not delegated aspects of the role of the priest, but directly held by the laity (*SC*, 29). It had been the practice of the church from the late Middle Ages that the celebrating priest was required to either perform or co-perform every action of the Mass, thus suggesting that the validity of these actions depended upon the priest doing them. Article 29 turns this situation around. The baptized have definite roles as liturgical ministers, as well as their role as the assembly.

It is no exaggeration to say that before the council baptism had sunk to a pitiful place and condition in the church's life. Baptism was something required by law to take place "*quam primum*" ("as soon as possible") —very shortly after birth—and the event was more or less entirely focused on the removal of original sin and, in the minds of many, the avoidance of limbo should the child die.[14] Lost to popular awareness was the New Testament sense of the baptized as "a new creation" in Christ, clothed with immortality, sharing in the dignity of the risen Lord. For all practical purposes, the baptized were treated as "poor banished children of Eve" just as much after baptism as they had been before. To speak of participation in the liturgy as the right and duty of the baptized therefore reasserted a value based on the tradition that had been sorely neglected.

Another aspect of ecclesiology treated succinctly in the document, yet significant to its overall vision, is the role of the bishop. The local church gathers around its bishop. The liturgy celebrated by the bishop in the cathedral church, with all the orders of clergy and laity present, is the norm of the Eucharist. The thinking of the document on this point is taken from Ignatius of Antioch. It is summed up in articles 41–42, and is also explored in article 26, which discusses the liturgy as the action of the whole church, hierarchically ordered.

What is a parish, then? According to the document, parishes are an accommodation to need. They can help people connect to the normative vision of the church that is expressed by the ordered assembly of people and clergy gathered around their bishop (*SC*, 42). The bishop cannot be everywhere, and so there are parishes. Contrary to popular assumption, however, the parish is not the local church. The local church is the diocese. The document harmonizes the differing roles of diocese and parish by emphasizing in both a "sense of community" found especially in the celebration of Eucharist.

The image of the bishop presiding at Eucharist with his presbyterate and all of the local church gathered around him in an ordered whole challenges the acceptance of a functional congregationalism of the parish. Because in today's large dioceses the bishop is often a distant figure—more like a CEO presiding over a bureaucracy than the quintessential presider over the Eucharistic banquet—the proper understanding of the role of the bishop cannot be taken for granted. The document softens its presentation by warm references to parishes, but still, the bishop's role presiding at the Eucharist in his cathedral is of primary symbolic significance.

Finally, by asserting that liturgy is a communal action, normally involving a congregation, and always an action of the church as a whole, not a private or individual function, the document firmly grounds the liturgical renewal in the idea of the church as the People of God. What emerges from the constitution as a primary image of church is the liturgical assembly, ordered and existing as an organic unity in all its members, with Christ as its head.

5. Inculturation

Articles 37 through 40 voice commitment to inculturation and the adaptation of the liturgy to the genius of diverse peoples throughout the world. The council opted for "substantial unity" rather than formal unity or uniformity in how the church worships. Further implications of these articles can be found in the sections on initiation (*SC*, 65), marriage (*SC*, 77), Christian burial (*SC*, 81), the liturgical year (*SC*, 107), penitential practices (*SC*, 110), music (*SC*, 119), and art (*SC*, 123). This commitment to inculturation of the liturgy is outstanding, and new.

Other great liturgical reforms of history—the Carolingian reform of the ninth century and the Tridentine reform of the sixteenth—had not taken this tack. They were centralizing reforms, aimed at establishing uniformity of practice. Vatican II did not abandon the centralizing tendency altogether, to be sure. The Holy See retained full power to approve or reject any adaptations of the liturgy, and the constitution stressed the point that no individual priest or anyone else may change the liturgy on his own initiative. Nevertheless, the document concedes in principle that the liturgy will not look the same in every place, and indeed invites the development of diverse practices corresponding to unique cultural contexts. Furthermore, it gives a novel role to territorial bodies of bishops (aided by experts) in taking responsibility for cultural adaptations of the liturgy.

The background to understanding these paragraphs lies in two separate areas: liturgical history and missions. The rise, before the council, of historical study of the liturgy made it clear that the rites of the church have always known diversity. Many rites have existed, and co-existed, with legitimate claims to the authority of tradition, from the earliest times. During the first centuries of Christian history, the churches of Europe, of North Africa, of Asia Minor, and of the Middle East each enjoyed distinctive liturgical traditions. Their liturgical diversity was no barrier to unity.

Diversity in liturgical practice persisted through the Middle Ages. Consider the famous correspondence between Saint Augustine of Canterbury and Pope Saint Gregory the Great (who reigned from 590 to 604), recorded in the Venerable Bede's *Ecclesiastical History of the English People*:

> *Augustine's Second Question:* Since we hold the same Faith, why do customs vary in different Churches? Why, for instance, does the method of saying Mass differ in the holy Roman Church and in the Churches of Gaul?

The sage reply of Pope Gregory shows no undue anxiety about the existence of multiple liturgical practices. These provide, in his view, a wealth of riches, by means of which genuine evangelization may prosper.

> *Pope Gregory's reply:* My brother, you are familiar with the usage of the Roman Church in which you were brought up. But if you have found customs, whether in the Roman, Gallican, or any other Churches that may be more acceptable to God, I wish you to make a careful selection of them, and teach the Church of the English, which is still young in the Faith, whatever you can profitably learn from the various Churches. For things should not be loved for the sake of places, but places for the

sake of good things. Therefore select from each of the Churches whatever things are devout, religious, and right; and when you have arranged them into a unified rite, let the minds of the English grow accustomed to it.[15]

Indeed, the co-existence of diverse liturgical practices was a fact of life for most of the church's history, despite centralizing tendencies. With the advent of the printing press, however (invented in the mid-fifteenth century), liturgical uniformity became attainable on a whole new scale. The coincidence of the liturgical reforms of Trent with the availability of the new technology of the printing press created an unprecedented situation. For the first time, the church in all parts of the globe could work from the same liturgical texts. The move toward standardization was strong and sweeping.[16] Liturgical variants were suppressed, unless they belonged to communities that wielded sufficient power to preserve their distinctive identities in local assemblies (by, for example, preserving liturgical practices specific to certain religious families, or to ancient sees).

The growth of world missions coincided with this period of the standardization of liturgical practice. Virtually no freedom to develop the liturgical genius of indigenous communities was given from Rome during the four-hundred-year span of the Tridentine era. Even with respect to the catechumenate and the administration of adult baptism—a subject of great pastoral concern for the missions—accommodation to diverse pastoral situations was severely limited until shortly before the Second Vatican Council.[17] This is precisely the situation that articles 37–40 of the constitution set out to address.

How, after so many years of enforced conformity, could liturgical diversity begin to seem acceptable again? One might point to positive changes in the general attitudes of Europeans toward non-European societies. With the rise of the social sciences in the twentieth century, a new appreciation of the value of distinctive human cultures around the globe had emerged. New developments in papal teaching in the decades immediately prior to the council likewise cleared the way for change in this arena. Finally, it is perhaps not too farfetched to say that the church had learned something from its negative historical experiences in imposing uniformity.

The story of the "Chinese rites controversy" provides a kind of historical parable that may help illustrate why the church of the Second

Vatican Council pursued the path that it did. This story begins with the phenomenal success of the sixteenth-century Jesuit missionary to China, Matteo Ricci. In many of the church's missionary settings, cultured Europeans had felt hitherto that they were bringing the gospel to primitive peoples, and therefore did not hesitate to dismiss their culture and customs. In China, however, missionaries were confronted with a cultured and learned civilization that was older than that of Europe and in many ways highly sophisticated. A different, more nuanced, and more respectful encounter seemed appropriate. Matteo Ricci was not the first to experience this challenge, but he rose to distinction through his skillful way of meeting it.

Ricci made numerous converts at the Chinese court and among the educated classes, who were fascinated by his learned discussion of religious issues as well as by the Western science and mathematics that he brought them. Ricci viewed Confucianism as a philosophy and set of social customs, not a religion, and so did not require the Chinese to abandon it upon becoming Christian.

The famous instruction of 1659 by the Sacred Congregation of Propaganda supported this approach wholeheartedly:

> Use no zeal, put forward no argument to convince these peoples to change their rites, customs and habits unless they are obviously contrary to religion and morality. What could be more absurd than to transport France, Spain, Italy or some other European country, among the Chinese? Do not bring them our countries, but our faith—that faith which *does not repel or wound the rites* or customs of any people, unless they are detestable, but on the contrary, wants them to be kept and protected.[18]

Opposition to Ricci's tolerant policies, however, arose among Franciscans and Dominicans and certain Jesuits, and they lobbied hard in Rome for a policy like the one they had pursued in Latin America, requiring complete rejection of indigenous customs. This party won.

When Pope Clement XI in 1715 demanded that Chinese Catholics renounce all associations with Confucianism and rites traditionally practiced to honor ancestors, disaster soon followed. Despite attempts at reconciliation by the Chinese, two hundred years of flourishing Christian missionary effort in China were undone by papal intransigence.

By 1742, Christianity had been banned, Westerners had been expelled, and the influx of Western science and technology to China had ceased. A hundred years of isolation ensued, to the detriment of both China and Europe. It was not until 1939 that the Papal Bull of 1715 was finally lifted—by none other than Pope Pius XII.

It was the first year of his pontificate. In that same year, Pope Pius XII produced his first encyclical, *Summi Pontificatus*, in which he wrote of the missions: "All that in such [varied civilizations'] usages and customs is not inseparably bound up with religious errors will always be subject to kindly consideration and, when it is found possible, will be sponsored and developed" (*SP*, 46). Pope Pius XII returned to this theme and expanded upon it at length in a later encyclical, *Evangelii Praecones* (1951). Pope John XXIII also took up the idea with enthusiasm in his encyclical of 1959, *Princeps Pastorum:*

> The Church, however, which is so full of youthful vigor and is constantly renewed by the breath of the Holy Spirit, is willing, at all times, to recognize, welcome, and even assimilate anything that redounds to the honor of the human mind and heart, whether or not it originates in parts of the world washed by the Mediterranean Sea, which, from the beginning of time, had been destined by God's Providence to be the cradle of the Church. (*PP*, 19)

This passage, quoted in *Princeps Pastorum*, was first delivered by the pope in a speech at the Second World Congress of Negro Writers and Artists in the summer of 1959; respect for cultural diversity was not limited to relations with the Chinese. In the very next paragraph of the encyclical, however, the pope adds an admiring reference to Matteo Ricci.

Because of the rise in awareness of cultural diversity since the time of the council—in civil society, education, and so on—some may assume that this principle was intended to be broader in scope than it actually was. Inculturation was not, for example, the umbrella under which the discussion of "use of the mother tongue" in liturgy took place. Latin and the vernacular were placed under the rubric of updating the church's liturgy to modern times, not that of accommodating the liturgy to the genius of diverse peoples.

In yet another way, the scope of these articles is narrower than one might think today. Inculturation of the liturgy was simply not considered an issue for the West at all. At the time of the council the focus was on adapting the liturgy to non-Western cultures in mission lands.

6. Renewal of the Liturgical Books, Music, Art, and Artifacts of the Liturgy

A complete overhaul of the church's liturgical books was commanded by the constitution. The Mass, the sacraments and sacramentals, the Divine Office or Liturgy of the Hours, and the liturgical year would all be reformed. Rites of religious profession and rites of burial were likewise included. The one sacrament that the preparatory commission had not recommended for discussion was penance. The commission felt that the council fathers would not understand the issues implicit in such a reform. A brief article was added, however, and thus, in the end, all the sacraments were included.[19] The renewal of church music, architecture, and all the artifacts of the liturgy was likewise set in motion by the constitution.

The council did not do the work of reform, but rather set the norms by which the work would be done and gave some specific instructions, such as the restoration of the prayer of the faithful, the extension of provisions for concelebration, and permission for communion under both forms. Without actually setting a timetable, it also created expectations for the time frame within which the reform would be accomplished. The liturgical reform was not an instance when the Roman dictum "we think in centuries here" would apply. The fathers originally wanted to see all the reforms completed in five years, but they agreed instead to say "as soon as possible" with the same idea in mind.[20]

General Norms

The general norms for the reform of the sacred liturgy are few in number; there are only four of them (*SC*, 22–25). They are (1) The reform is based on the authority of the church; (2) it is to be undertaken in conformity with sound tradition, rightly judged and interpreted; (3) it is to be imbued with sacred scripture; and (4) it is to be accomplished efficiently, with all relevant expertise, both practical and pastoral.

The first norm, found in article 22, is of great significance to establishing the legitimacy of the project and its orderly implementation. It asserts that regulation of the liturgy belongs to church authority: the pope and, where appropriate, the bishops. Territorial bodies of bishops may also play a role. Nobody else, not even a priest, has the authority to tamper with the liturgy. Thus later, when Archbishop Lefèbvre decided to reject the reformed liturgy, he was ruled out of court. Autonomous individual "experimenters" of the post-conciliar period, so often caricatured as the offspring of the reform, are likewise repudiated by the norms of the constitution itself.

What may be the most interesting assertion of this article in the long run is the provision for territorial bodies of bishops to assume a role in the regulation of the liturgy. Such bodies are a plausible construction for practical reasons, but they have no great anchor in tradition. In terms of power politics, they represent a middle ground between the pope and any individual bishop, and thus become the place where a balance needs to be negotiated between central authority and regional needs. This—predictably—is a messy and vulnerable business, threatening always to malfunction or even disintegrate when there are conflicts between the two. Yet the decision to involve territorial bodies of bishops in liturgical decisions exhibits a certain wisdom about how the liturgy flourishes. It is best that the liturgy not be shaped either by the individual bishop alone, or by the Holy See alone, or even by a combination of the two. Geographical areas larger than a diocese and smaller than the universal church ought to be taken into account simply because society is organized this way. By calling for collegiality among bishops, this provision also draws on some of the church's best impulses of collaboration and charity among pastoral leaders.

The second general norm, article 23, concerns tradition. Careful theological, historical, and pastoral study is to ground the liturgical reform. Recent experience with legitimate experimentation too must be consulted. The reform was never intended to sweep away the past and begin with a blank slate, as this paragraph bears witness. Both the retention of "sound tradition" and the achievement of "legitimate progress" are its stated goals. In fact, novelty is never to be pursued for its own sake, but changes are to be implemented only when they are for the benefit of the faithful. The article states that "there are to be no innovations unless the good of the Church genuinely and certainly requires them." It is clearly accepted that there will be innovations, however, because the very same sentence goes on to say that "new forms" should "grow organically" from "forms already existing." Finally, neighboring regions should strive to keep their rites similar, presumably to avoid excessive localization of liturgical practice.

The value placed on "sound tradition" here is very important, and frequently misunderstood. Not everything inherited from the past constitutes "sound tradition." Some liturgical practices are moribund and deserve to be buried. They arose in response to circumstances and needs that no longer exist.

There are numerous instances of this. One rather amusing example is the use of the maniple, an ornate, usually silk, band of cloth decorated with embroidered crosses, and sometimes with fringes and bells, affixed to the left arm. This was worn by several orders of clergy, but was the special vesture of the subdeacon (one of the minor orders, suppressed after the council). Originally this bit of cloth had a practical purpose. It was a pocket-handkerchief to wipe away sweat. Through the centuries, however, the maniple had somehow come to symbolize "the bonds that Christ bore" on the way to his crucifixion. The use of such a vestment— fussy, theologically confused, linked to sumptuous display, and lacking any real function (actual pocket handkerchiefs being available)—was left behind in the reform.

Another example is the reading of the so-called "Last Gospel" at the end of Mass. This reading, the prologue of Saint John's Gospel, was originally a private devotion of the priest, to be said after Mass. A pious practice that had grown up in the Middle Ages, the reading of the prologue of John's Gospel was seen as a kind of blessing. It entered the liturgy for the first time in the twelfth century. The Tridentine reform made this private reading public and obligatory. It also allowed other gospels to be read at the end of Mass from time to time. An elaborate method of deciding which would be read, depending on the saint's day, was in force until Pope Pius XII simplified the rubrics in 1955.

The reformers of Vatican II had to face the fact that nobody thinks of the prologue of Saint John's Gospel as a blessing any longer. And even if anyone does think of it as a blessing, Mass already concludes with a blessing. Eliminating "useless repetitions" was part of the constitution's program (*SC*, 34). Theological embroideries, added long after the fact, did not alter the basic situation.[21] Although the prologue of John's Gospel is a very beautiful passage of scripture, its placement at the end of the Eucharist was simply incoherent, and so this practice too was dropped.

On the other hand, there are liturgical practices—some very ancient—that possess a vibrant power to enliven faith and deepen the worshippers' adherence to Christ. Immersion in the waters of baptism, anointing with oil, laying on of hands, and various forms of prayer are but a few examples of such ancient elements of rite that survive splendidly to the present day. They serve genuine liturgical functions. They carry the weight of true and lasting tradition and must by all means be preserved.

Only by careful and painstaking study does clarity about genuine tradition emerge. In some cases disagreement may very well exist about whether a certain element is essential or peripheral, subject to change or not. There is simply no getting around the fact that individual evaluations and judgments have to be made by the authorities gathered to make such judgments, enlightened by the help of relevant experts. Hence the continuing importance of article 22: the regulation of the liturgy belongs to the authority of the church. If everyone who has an opinion about what constitutes genuine tradition "writes his own ticket," soon there will be no common liturgy at all.

If the problem of what constitutes sound tradition is tricky, so too is the question of how new forms "grow organically" from old ones, given the fact that the revisions of the rites are expected to take place within a very short time frame. Organic growth usually presumes generations, one would think—a kind of gradual evolution. Given the legal approach to liturgical change embodied in the document, however, it seems unlikely that the council actually had in mind those changes that take place "naturally" (i.e., without permission), as most "organic" processes do. One might well wonder what this provision really means.

The point being made here is admittedly rather vague ("in some way") and metaphorical ("grow"), but it makes a certain amount of sense when viewed in context. Perhaps a couple of examples can help flesh it out. Take, for instance, the renewal of baptismal promises practiced in the Easter Vigil, as it was restored by Pope Pius XII in 1951, with which all the fathers at the council would have been familiar. The renewal of baptismal promises was never before seen in the Roman Missal. It was "new." But there was a practice in the ancient church—the *"Pascha Annotinum"*—of marking the anniversary of baptism on Low Sunday, by saying the Creed. The "organic" connection between this ancient precedent and the new form it took lay not in an uninterrupted historical continuance, but rather in the recognition of an inner logic that inspired both practices.[22] The new form was very successful and, although new, it was not "untraditional"—as it would be to baptize with rose petals, for instance. A similar argument could be made for the washing of feet on Holy Thursday, first implemented in 1955. As a liturgical gesture it can be found historically in various other settings (monasteries, cathedrals, etc.) on diverse occasions. It was new to its place in the liturgy of Holy Thursday, but not new to the church. Because it mirrors the scriptures of that liturgy and has a keenly relevant pastoral purpose, the ritual of foot washing after the gospel does exhibit a kind of organic connection with the Mass of the Lord's Supper.

On the other hand, an example of a new practice that stemmed more obviously from then-current forms but was less successful can be found within the reform of the Mass. The penitential rite incorporated into the opening rites of the Mass was new to the people. But it came directly from the prayers at the foot of the altar formerly said by the priest and ministers. The two practices have a close connection, to be sure, but still the rite is "new." The penitential rite in the Mass of Paul VI has been criticized by liturgists after the council as inappropriate and burdensome to the opening rites. But is it an organic development, hence traditional in a good sense? Through a particular set of lenses, yes. Through others, it may seem not at all "organic" to have the people do something that used to be done by the priest and ministers. Still others would argue that the problem here is that penance is not an organic part of the Eucharist, period, and the whole thing ought to have been relinquished from the beginning. Thus the discussion goes on, without the principle of organic development providing easy answers. How the church determines sound tradition and fosters its development continues to be an area where disputes may arise.

The third of the general norms concerns scripture. The document says that "Sacred scripture is of the greatest importance in the celebration of the liturgy.... Thus to achieve the restoration, progress, and adaptation of the sacred liturgy, it is essential to promote that warm and living love for scripture to which the venerable tradition of both eastern and western rites gives testimony" (*SC*, 24).

The constitution can be read in conjunction with the council document on scripture, *Dei Verbum*, to give a fuller sense of what this norm portended. But even if the spotlight is limited to the question of scripture in the liturgy, one can see that a principle of great consequence is being introduced here. It signals several practical developments. Scripture readings will be selected to accompany every Mass and every sacrament. The Liturgy of the Hours too will have more abundant readings from scripture (*SC*, 92a). More readings will be introduced into the Sunday Lectionary for Mass, and a complete weekday lectionary with ample scriptural readings will also be put in place (*SC*, 51). There is to be more frequent preaching, and preachers are to be instructed that the content of preaching be drawn from scripture and the liturgy itself (*SC*, 35.2, 52).

In looking back on the reforms of Vatican II, Father Pierre Jounel, a liturgical scholar and peritus at the council (he also worked on the preparatory commission), commented favorably on the implementation of this general norm. He remarked in a 1994 interview that:

> The thing that has worked best, it seems to me, is the recovery of the proclamation of the word of God as a structural element in all liturgical celebrations. "The book is the chalice," said John XXIII. Everyone today is convinced of the truth of this. No sacrament is celebrated today without being preceded by a reading from the Word of God. This was an absolute novelty in the Roman liturgy, hence the importance of lectionaries for Mass, for the sacraments, for the Liturgy of the Hours.[23]

Many others, in looking back on the council, would agree. The quantity of scripture available in the liturgy would grow immensely as the result of the reform and be taken much more to heart as the renewal of the liturgy progressed.

Due to the intervention of two Argentine bishops, Jorge Kemerer and Alberto Devoto, provision also was added for word services apart from the Mass or the sacraments (*SC*, 35.4)—thus going beyond the plan of the preparatory commission and reestablishing a practice from apostolic times. The motivation here was not ecumenism, but rather to respond to contemporary needs in areas where the priest shortage was keen.[24]

The fourth and final general norm concerns the time frame of the reform and the expertise required to conduct it. This very brief paragraph (*SC*, 25) has several noteworthy elements. The expression "as soon as possible" was expected to mean something in the vicinity of five years. The reference to experts affirms what was earlier said about the need for thorough and careful study of the tradition and current experience. Because considerable research had been going on for years before the council, such expertise did not need to be developed from scratch. It is also worth noting that the council easily and coolly accepted expertise from non-bishops. There seems to be no hint of suspicion concerning such expertise, nor threat of being overwhelmed by it. It was obvious that scholars, linguists, historians, theologians, and others would be needed for the work of liturgical reform. Finally, bishops "from various parts of the world" are to be consulted. Actual pastoral experience on the ground, in all parts of the globe, should go into the making of the liturgical reform. The bishops would be active collaborators in the effort, not merely consumers of a product prepared for them.

Characteristics of the Reform

Without going through each and every item in the rest of the document, we will take a look at some of its key assertions about how the liturgy is to be reformed.

Liturgical Services Are Not Private Functions

Community participation in the liturgy is a central concern of the document. Without ruling out private celebrations absolutely, the document takes great pains to assert that communal celebrations are always to be preferred (*SC*, 27). When the people are present, they serve in genuine liturgical functions (*SC*, 29), their participation is to be encouraged by every possible means (*SC*, 30), and their parts are to be written into the rubrics of the revised books (*SC*, 31). No special honors are to be given to private persons or classes of people, aside from the distinctions arising from the church's orders, liturgical functions, and lawfully determined considerations for civil authorities (*SC*, 32). Thus the liturgy emerges as a gathering of the people of God, first and foremost.

Noble Simplicity

Under the rubric of the "pastoral and didactic" nature of the liturgy, the constitution enunciates a principle that will be used to determine many questions concerning how the liturgy will be reformed. It says "The rites should be distinguished by a noble simplicity; they should be short, clear, and unencumbered by useless repetitions; they should be within the people's power of comprehension and normally should not require much explanation" (*SC*, 34).

This paragraph and the reform overall were influenced by the observations of Edmund Bishop (1846–1917), in whose seminal essay "The Genius of the Roman Rite" the term "noble simplicity" first appeared.[25] The Roman rite, as opposed to other ritual usages, has from its earliest history been marked by "sobriety and a lack of excess" in its prayers and gestures. Indeed, the Latin language itself is well adapted to saying a lot in very few words, and by comparison to other rites, the Roman rite is sparing of gesture and limited in ritual repetition. Where it departs from this standard, the elements in question usually can be traced to other sources. The council was concerned to protect the genuine character of the Roman rite while reforming it.

The desideratum that the liturgy should not normally require a lot of explanation does not mean that catechesis is unnecessary, or that banal language is preferable to exalted language in prayer. What this paragraph is trying to suppress, rather, is mystification for its own sake. God's truth is simple. It is filled with deep mystery, but this is not because humans have constructed a bewildering maze of archaisms around it. Sadly, it is possible for liturgy to evolve into something that resembles magic, replete with all the glamour of secret incantations and gestures that suggest something fearful and forbidden, yet alluring and powerful. The experience of liturgy should not be like that because the faith of the church is not like that. The gospel Jesus preached was good news, not gnosticism. The God whom Jesus revealed has made himself accessible to the poor, the unlettered, and "the merest children" (Matt 11:25). Worship therefore must not be so constructed that it becomes an activity confined to an elite.

As with other assertions of the document, the implementation of this principle required a host of concrete decisions to be made. These would subsequently be disputed. On one side of the principle of noble simplicity there is mystification to be avoided. On the other there is the danger of "dumbing down" the liturgy. Religious language is freighted with complex meaning, requires explanation, and even then may preserve nuances that elude its hearers until grasped through much repetition, meditation, and conversion of heart. This is true of the language of the scriptures and of the great fund of liturgical prayer texts handed down through the ages. It is also true of the "language" of ritual itself. The poetry of prayer, symbols that speak in multivalent ways, gestures and postures of importance to worship might all seem to be at risk if the litmus test is "comprehension." Shouldn't the liturgy lead us to God himself, who always stands beyond the human power to comprehend? Celebrating a liturgy, after all, is not like reading a newspaper. In short, the path opened up by this principle would take much wisdom to chart.

Latin and the Vernacular

In article 36.1, the constitution says clearly that "the use of the Latin language is to be preserved in the Latin rites." The next paragraph (36.2), however, states that use of "the mother tongue" in the Mass, the sacraments, and so on, may be extended. Readings, directives, and some of the prayers and chants are envisioned. Article 54 again mentions the readings and also the prayer of the faithful and "those parts which pertain to the people" as sections of the liturgy that might potentially be celebrated in the vernacular.

There were strong feelings at the council on both sides of the question of whether vernacular languages should be permitted in the liturgy, and the document reflects both points of view. A cautious, limited possibility was held out for some use of the mother tongue, but the use of Latin as the language of the liturgy for the Latin rite churches was affirmed. This was surely a compromise, because the fathers of the council were not in agreement.[26] Those who favored Latin saw in it a crucial expression of the unity of the Latin rite church, and a guarantee of orthodoxy. Those who favored the vernacular believed it to be essential to the expression and cultivation of the living faith of the people, for whom Latin was no longer a living language. Father Columba Kelly, OSB, who was a student in Rome at the time of the council, recalls one of his teachers, Annibale Bugnini, telling his class, of the two differing tendencies, that "[w]e want both of those in there so that history will take care of how to balance the two."[27]

By all accounts, history decided in favor of the mother tongue. The fathers of the council, however, did not expect the desire for celebration in the vernacular to rise so quickly or to be so overwhelming. Most felt the vernacular would not be needed for the Divine Office at all, and that Latin plainchant would always predominate in the area of liturgical music, even when alternatives were allowed.[28]

Communion under Both Forms

A profound and noteworthy change inaugurated by the constitution is the sharing of the chalice with the laity. The document also warmly commends the faithful who receive from the same sacrifice as the priest but, as we saw earlier, this was not in any way a new proposal. The permission to share communion under both forms with the laity, on the other hand, was a landmark decision, making concrete the idea of participation in an especially important way.

Communion under both forms corresponds to the Lord's command, and is a tradition from apostolic times. It had been standard practice in the history of the church up to the Middle Ages, when the taking of communion became more infrequent. A gradual decline in the sharing of the chalice ultimately led to communion under one form being the general practice. Finally, from the thirteenth century onward, the chalice was restricted to the priest alone. The limiting of communion to one form was defended at the Council of Trent on the grounds that Christ is fully present in communion under either the form of bread or of wine. Both forms always had to be present in the Mass for validity, but the cup was not shared.

For those who discount the sharing of communion under both forms as merely an aesthetic issue, it is good to remember the Utraquists of Bohemia (the area that is now the Czech Republic) and their spiritual leader, Jan Hus, who in 1415 was burned at the stake as a heretic for, among other things, refusing to give up the chalice. (The name Utraquist comes from the Latin for communion under both forms: *sub utraque specie*.) Indeed the historic refusal of the Catholic Church to share the chalice with the laity had for centuries been a cause for reproach by Christians not in communion with Rome. Martin Luther had advocated communion from the cup in his polemical work *The Babylonian Captivity of the Church* (1520), and other reformers of the sixteenth century followed suit. Restriction of the chalice to the priest was also a mark of division between Rome and the churches of the East, which had preserved intact the ancient practice of communion under both forms.

The opening up of this possibility therefore accomplished, at least in principle, two goals. First, it invigorated the church's experience of Holy Communion by reviving the fullness of the sign. Second, the sharing of communion under both forms removed a barrier to ecumenism.

Although the provision does not change the teaching of Trent that Christ is fully present under each form, it is a step in the direction of unity with Christians of both the East and the West.

In the document, the examples of when communion might be offered in this way are once-in-a-lifetime events. Thus the measure is very cautious. This reflects the fact that the fathers were divided on the question. During the discussion on the Eucharist, this provision generated the most disagreement, after language and concelebration, with some wishing more broad endorsement, additional instances, and so on, and others determined in their opposition.[29] Those who opposed a broader usage of the cup were mollified by the fact that the instances named were few, while those who favored it were assured that the actual permission could be far broader if local bishops wanted to avail themselves of it.

Preservation and Renewal of Music and Art

In music, art, and architecture, the document advises appreciating and preserving works of the past, while inviting new artistic expressions fit for divine worship and suitable for the reformed liturgy.

In sacred music, the constitution instructs, Gregorian chant is to be preferred, other things being equal, because it is uniquely suited to the Roman liturgy (*SC*, 116). The document affirms that the pipe organ is also especially honored in the churches of the Latin rite, although other instruments may be used (*SC*, 120). The church's patrimony of sacred music is to be preserved and choirs cherished, though not at the expense of the people singing the parts that are rightly theirs (*SC*, 114). New musical compositions are welcomed (*SC*, 121).

Preference is given to singing the texts of scripture and the liturgy itself (*SC*, 121). Indeed "sacred music is to be considered the more holy in proportion as it is more closely connected with the liturgical action..." (*SC*, 112). This important principle would later result in a great flourishing of so-called "ritual music" as opposed to music as artwork adorning the occasion but not forwarding the liturgical action.

In sacred art, likewise, the church's treasury of artwork is to be carefully discerned and preserved. New art from "every race and region" is welcomed, provided it brings "reverence and honor" to the buildings and rites it adorns (*SC*, 123). In an expression analogous to the principle of "noble simplicity" that belongs to the rites themselves, the document says that bishops should promote art characterized by "noble beauty rather than sumptuous display" in vestments, ornaments, and artworks (*SC*, 124).

Bishops are also instructed to get rid of artworks that are "repugnant to faith, morals, and Christian piety." In this realm, no half measures will do. Anything that offends "true religious sense" by "lack of artistic worth, mediocrity and pretense" is to be removed (*SC*, 124).

New guidelines are to be written for the construction of churches, including laws that bring churches and their furnishings into conformity with the reformed liturgy. These will concern the shape and construction of altars, "nobility, placing, and safety" of the tabernacle, suitable and dignified baptisteries, as well as the "proper ordering" of images, "embellishments," and vestments (*SC*, 128).

7. Education and Formation

The human material, so to speak, that goes into the making of the liturgy is also given due attention by the constitution. In order for the deep and wide-ranging reform of the liturgy to take place, there must be intelligent and active support for change at every level in the church. How will such knowledgeable and willing cooperation be cultivated? The constitution calls for thoroughgoing efforts at education and formation.

The document concentrates on the education and formation of clergy and religious, first of all. Professors of liturgy to teach in seminaries must be trained (*SC*, 15). The study of liturgy should be among the compulsory and major courses of study in seminaries (*SC*, 16). The constitution also asks that other disciplines, such as theology and scripture, support and complement the study of liturgy (*SC*, 16). It directs that, in addition to courses on liturgy, liturgical formation be provided in seminaries and religious houses as part of training in the spiritual life (*SC*, 17). It eloquently pleads with pastors to become imbued with the spirit of the liturgy, and to grow in their own knowledge of it, so as to be able to pass on an informed love for the liturgy effectively to their people (*SC*, 14, 18–19).

Ministers of sacred music are to be given liturgical formation as well as musical training (*SC*, 115), and bishops are responsible for guiding and supporting the formation of artists too (*SC*, 127). To assist in the implementation of the norms of the constitution in the areas of music and the arts, commissions concerning them are to be set up (*SC*, 46). These will help cultivate appropriate liturgical education and formation in their respective areas. Both territorial and diocesan liturgical commissions are called for by the constitution (*SC*, 44, 45), and asked to work closely with the commissions devoted to music and the arts. They are to help the diocesan bishop(s) to foster and regulate the liturgy on a local level.

Although structures of lay formation and education are not discussed in the document, the desired outcomes of lay formation are stated throughout the entire work. The faithful are to be active and conscious participants in the liturgy. They are to understand the words and actions of the liturgy, and indeed the very mystery the liturgy celebrates. A warm and living love for scripture is to characterize their devout participation. With regard to the Eucharist, they are to understand the liturgy's parts and their interrelationship, and they are to be taught to come to the whole Mass (*SC*, 56).[30] The liturgy teaches, the document asserts, and so participation in the liturgy is itself formative and educational (*SC*, 33).

CONCLUSION

The Constitution on the Sacred Liturgy proposed an ambitious agenda for the church. As a constitution, the document is permanent law. It concerns disciplinary matters, and as such it had both an immediate and long-lasting effect on liturgical practice. The document was the culmination of a long process that led up to its writing. At the same time, it was only the beginning. It set forth expectations to be fulfilled by many others in the years to come. In the next chapter we will see how this agenda fared following the council.

PART III

IMPLEMENTATION

Even before the Second Vatican Council was over, the reform of the liturgy called for by *Sacrosanctum Concilium* began to be carried out. There was no question that changes would take place. The charter for great changes, as we have seen, was provided by the constitution itself. The council fathers had decided in favor of a profound reform and called for its rapid execution. They gave direction, and the work of implementation passed into other hands.

The situation on the ground was far from simple. Local churches in some parts of the world, such as the Netherlands and parts of France and Germany, were bursting with enthusiasm for change. Local bishops struggled to keep on top of situations that were fast slipping out of their control, as priests ran ahead of the reform and unauthorized prayers and rites proliferated. At the same time, more moderate desire for an updating of the liturgy had been rising in many places around the globe, and a welcome was ready for the new developments brought by the council. Some church leaders remained skeptical, but were willing to go with the reform. Others were determined to resist it. At the far end of the spectrum, ultraconservatives decried the entire Second Vatican Council as a freemasonic plot, maligned anyone associated with the liturgical reform, and attacked teachings of the council across the board.[1] Those in the Vatican bureaucracy who had not wanted liturgical change in the first place remained in power, even as the machinery of the council's implementation ground into gear.

THE MAKING OF THE REFORMED LITURGY: 1963–1975

A post-conciliar commission on the liturgy was appointed by the Holy See to carry out the directives of the council. Its work, done in close collaboration with Pope Paul VI, spanned the years from 1964 to 1969. Its name was *Consilium ad exsequendam Constitutionem de sacra Liturgia.* In English this body is usually referred to as "the Consilium" which means "deliberative body" or "council," but is not to be confused with the Second Vatican Council itself. It was made up of about 50 cardinals and bishops (members) and 150 experts in liturgy and related fields (consultors) who labored alongside one another throughout the work, with little regard for who was a member and who was not. This body was a veritable "who's who" of contemporary liturgical scholarship, pastoral experience, and expertise in related fields such as languages, scripture, and history, drawn from all over the world. Almost all the members were priests, and many belonged to religious communities. There were a few lay consultors, however, and one was a woman: Professor Christine Mohrmann of the Netherlands, an expert on Christian Latin.

The Consilium was separate from the curial agency, the Congregation of Rites, that was responsible for liturgical regulation. The two were linked (the work of the Consilium was disseminated via the congregation), but they were never close. The Consilium existed in parallel to the Congregation of Rites, and by reporting directly to the pope could exercise a degree of autonomy with respect to the congregation. This allowed it the freedom to carry on its work in ways that were best suited to its task, through study groups and interdisciplinary consultation. But there was potential for rivalry between the congregation and the Consilium.

Internal to the workings of the Consilium itself there were the normal differences of opinion and differing views concerning how the work should be done, as might be expected. But by all accounts there was great cooperation. Pope Paul VI approved of the work and for the most part did not meddle with it. He occasionally exercised his prerogative, however, to make a decision contrary to that of the majority.

Most of the Consilium, for example, took the conservative view that all 150 psalms should be prayed in the Liturgy of the Hours over the course of the four-week psalter. The pope, however, agreed with the minority opinion, which held it was not pastoral to include the so-called "imprecatory" psalms (psalms that curse Israel's enemies), and wanted also to limit the recitation of the historical psalms (psalms detailing

Israel's history) to certain seasons. Despite several discussions in which the subject was revisited, the pope's decision remained firm.

In another instance, it was due to the personal decision of the pope that the sign of the cross that begins the Mass would always be accompanied by words invoking the Trinity, with a response by the people. There were a number of arguments against this. It was not considered traditional for either the Latin rite or the Eastern rite churches (in the Byzantine rite, the gesture is done by the priest alone, in silence). In the Roman rite, it was done by the priest alone, and was part of the personal prayers of the priest at the foot of the altar; in sung Masses it used to take place during the singing, and thus was inaudible. (One of the working guidelines used by the Consilium was that the sung Mass, and not a low Mass, without music, would be considered the norm. Here, in effect, the new rite would be taking its cue from the low Mass.) Furthermore, to begin with this invocation of the Trinity would duplicate the Trinitarian formula of the greeting that immediately followed it. Finally, by having the sign of the cross after the opening song, it would make it appear that Mass was beginning a second time, when it had already begun with the song. The pope was not persuaded by these arguments, however, and the matter was decided in accordance with his wishes.

In yet another example, the pope made a choice that ran counter to the wisdom of the experts, and yet their response to his decision created a new and effective solution to a problem. Pope Paul VI decided to retain the words *"mysterium fidei"* ("the mystery of faith") in the canon of the Mass. The origins of the phrase are unknown. Its purpose in the Eucharistic Prayer was indeed puzzling, for it seemed quite disconnected with what came before and after it. When the Consilium was faced with the necessity of keeping the phrase, however, one of the periti, Father Joseph Gelineau, SJ, advanced the felicitous suggestion that it be used to introduce a sung acclamation in praise of the paschal mystery.[2] This course was adopted, with the result that now the meaning of *"mysterium fidei"* seems not only clear but obviously integral to the celebration.

The achievements of the Consilium were prodigious. In a short time great progress was made on the revision of the Roman Missal, the Lectionary for Mass, the Roman Ritual, and the Liturgy of the Hours. To review all the specifics would go far beyond the scope of this work.

But it must be noted that the general principles set forth in the constitution were meticulously followed. Participation of the people was written into every liturgical celebration. The liturgy as the work of the people, rather than of the priest alone, became evident. Pastoral options were included in abundance, and room for local decisions and adaptations was allowed. The rites were streamlined ("noble simplicity"), but at times also enriched. A very much expanded lectionary was devised, with a three-year cycle of readings for Sundays and a two-year cycle for weekdays. In every one of the revised liturgical books, the paschal mystery was brought to the fore. Priority was given to the liturgical action and its corporate expression. A token of the profound change in perspective that occurred as a result of the council can be found in first line of the rubrics for how Mass begins. The words in the old missal were: "The priest being ready..."; in the new: "The people having gathered..."

Most Catholics today are unaware of the very extensive work that went into the reform of the liturgical books. The composition of three alternative Eucharistic Prayers in addition to the old Roman canon, for example, was an outstanding accomplishment. The people who composed these texts drew from ancient liturgies and scriptural sources. They were able to address a very old problem of the Roman canon, a prayer which, strangely, did not explicitly call on the Holy Spirit. The new Eucharistic prayers now include an epiclesis, that is, they invoke the Spirit over the people and the gifts.[3]

The simplicity and clarity that all the liturgical rites of the church now enjoy was the fruit of careful pruning, each instance carefully researched. Almost as the colors of a painting emerge afresh when the dust of ages is removed from them by skilled art restorers, so the essential elements of each liturgy were made visible again by the work that went into their refurbishment.

The riches of scripture, now so lavishly shared in the liturgy, were presented in readings selected both to suit the individual celebration and to expose the faithful to books of the Bible in a course of semi-continuous readings carried on from week to week. The Old Testament is now frequently heard, along with the New, in the readings day by day.

All the sacraments were updated to address pastoral circumstances and needs. The rite for infant baptism, for example, was for the first time rewritten in light of the fact that the candidates are infants. It includes specific commitments to be made by parents and godparents to underscore their responsibility to bring up the child in the faith. The *Pastoral Care of the Sick* and the *Order of Christian Funerals* were enriched with many useful options, and were imbued with a paschal spirit. Marriage and ordination rites were revised to bring out their essential aspects more clearly.

Aside from the production of liturgical books in Rome, the reform was proceeding on other fronts as well. Permissions for use of the vernacular and for cultural adaptations of the liturgy were sought and obtained around the world. Commissions were formed to do the work of translation of official texts. For example, even before the end of the council, representatives of eleven English-speaking episcopal conferences had gotten together to plan a "mixed commission" (i.e., one drawn from multiple conferences) to produce English translations for liturgical use. This body, called the International Commission on English in the Liturgy (ICEL), was founded in 1963.

An instruction on the translation of texts, *Comme le prévoit*, was issued by the Vatican in 1969 to guide the work of translators. It regarded the question of inculturation as inextricable from the question of translation, and urged not only that texts be translated by the method known as "dynamic equivalence," but also that new original texts be written in the vernacular languages. In the English speaking world, provisional texts, mostly drawn from existing translations that had appeared previously in missals and such, were put into use as early as 1965. The ICEL translation of the Sacramentary, which had followed the principles of *Comme le prévoit*, was published in 1973.

In dioceses, bishops set up liturgical commissions and, in some cases, music and art commissions as well. An instruction on liturgical music, *Musicam Sacram*, was issued from Rome in 1967. It contained, among other things, some practical guidance about which parts of the Mass ought to be sung by the people. The idea of "progressive solemnity," which takes into account the difference between simple and more solemn liturgical events, was fleshed out with examples. An outstanding aspect of this instruction was the great emphasis it placed on the assembly singing *in dialogue* with the celebrant. This advice was often ignored, however. People preferred to sing familiar hymns or listen to a choir, and not every celebrant wanted to sing.

Settings of the psalms in the vernacular, such as those composed by Joseph Gelineau and Lucien Deiss, became popular, and service music for the vernacular liturgy appeared. By and large, when people recall the "new" music that appeared in parishes after the council, however, they do not think of psalms or settings of the Eucharistic Prayer or dialogue chants between the people and the celebrant. They recall, rather, those new songs that replaced the old devotional hymns. Thus "Little White Guest" and "Bring Flowers of the Fairest" gave way to "Kumbaya" and "Here We Are," but a more *liturgical* sense of music had yet to develop. Catholics were "singing at Mass," but still seldom "singing the Mass."

Educational institutions began to include liturgy in their curricula. Higher education in liturgy at first was concentrated in Europe, at institutes in Paris, Rome, and Trier. Americans trained in such European institutes established advanced programs of study, such as the ones at Notre Dame in Indiana and Catholic University in Washington, DC, in the 1960s. The introduction of trained liturgy faculty into seminaries and religious houses of study was not by any means universal, but efforts were made to improve the liturgical education of priests and religious.

Ecumenical work concerning the liturgy increased. One strategy of ecumenism with respect to worship is to increase the degree to which, even when communities worship separately, they are using the same prayers, rituals, and sacred texts, or at least ones that closely resemble each other. The International Consultation on English Texts (ICET), an ecumenical body, was formed to work jointly on key texts that could be used by Christians regardless of their denominational affiliation. It produced common translations of the Creed, the Lord's Prayer, and other liturgical texts. The North American partner association to ICET, the Consultation on Common Texts, produced an ecumenical adaptation of the Roman Lectionary called the Common Lectionary that is now used by Christian churches throughout the English-speaking world. Although never adopted by the Catholic Church, this lectionary has much in common with the Catholic lectionary and represents an important convergence in thought and practice.

There had been notable non-Catholic participation in the liturgical movement even before the time of the council, and with the accelerating reforms within the Catholic Church, the collaboration of scholars across denominational lines received a new impetus. One expression of this was the founding of *Societas Liturgica*, an international, ecumenical organization of liturgy scholars, begun in 1962 by Wiebe Vos of the Netherlands. Study of the liturgical sources in turn caused many ecclesial communities to reexamine their traditions. A return to practices such as weekly Eucharist or the common cup for example, traditions which for many Protestants had been lost, became possible in a number of denominations as a result of the liturgical renewal.

In the day-to-day life of Catholic parishes the world over, changes started to emerge. Pastors began to remove from churches artwork that they deemed unworthy or inappropriate, such as cheap statues or gaudy paintings. Side altars, now no longer used for multiple Masses, were either removed or turned into devotional spaces; in many churches altar rails were taken out as greater numbers of people stood to take communion. Pastors allowed new music in the liturgy. Use of the piano, which had been forbidden by Pope Pius X in *Tra le Sollecitudini* in 1903, was now permitted. Other instruments, such as guitars, began to be heard in church as well. A variety of lay ministers, such as readers, commentators, song leaders, and extraordinary ministers of Holy Communion—and these lay ministers included women—appeared in the sanctuary for the first time. Fasting regulations were eased, and in 1968 permission was given for Sunday Mass to be anticipated on Saturday evening. Women stopped wearing veils to church.

On the popular level, most people remember three things about their parish experience of the liturgy immediately following Vatican II: the use of the vernacular, changes in music and art, and the priest facing the people at Mass. The first two arise obviously from provisions found in the constitution itself. What about the third?

Experiments in celebrating the Mass with the priest facing the people had been tried as early as the 1920s and were received with great enthusiasm. Romano Guardini and Pius Parsch were in the vanguard of this experiment, which was undertaken as a pastoral initiative. The arrangement of the priest facing the people placed the sacred elements in the center, gave a clearer impression of the Eucharist as the meal instituted by Jesus, and led to increased engagement in the liturgical action taking place at the altar. The people around the altar saw themselves as the church gathered with Christ present in their midst.

Although the practice of the priest facing the people was not mentioned in the constitution itself, it was officially endorsed even before

the council ended, in 1964, by the first instruction on the proper implementation of the Constitution on the Sacred Liturgy, *Inter Oecumenici*.
On the basis of this instruction, it was written into the Roman Missal
that the altar should be freestanding, allowing the priest to walk around
it and to face the people. In 1965, a massive work by Professor Otto
Nussbaum was published, arguing that up until the sixth century it is
most likely that the position of the priest at the altar was facing the
people.[4] By and large, however, the change was introduced less for reasons of historical authenticity than for its pastoral benefits.

   Inter Oecumenici (1964) was the first of three instructions for the
right application of the conciliar constitution on the liturgy. The first
two appeared under the auspices of the Congregation of Rites, the third
under the Congregation for Divine Worship, all with the approval of
Pope Paul VI. The first addressed a host of small questions including
the placement of the tabernacle, side altars, and the like. It enumerated
parts of the liturgy that could be in the vernacular, directed the creation
of freestanding altars, and established the lawfulness of the priest celebrating Mass facing the people.

   The other two instructions were *Tres Abhinc Annos* (1967) and
Liturgicae Instaurationes (1970). *Tres Abhinc Annos* broadened the use of
the vernacular to include the canon of the Mass, the recitation of the
Hours, and all the rites of holy orders. It addressed a number of specific
questions regarding prayers of the priest and vesture (this is when the
maniple was retired) and exhorted obedience to lawfully established
liturgical norms for the harmony and good of the church. *Liturgicae
Instaurationes* reiterated the necessity of abolishing "improvisations" by
the individual priest, attended to questions about materials used in the
liturgy, specifically bread for the Eucharist and worthy communion ves-
sels, listed liturgical ministries open to women (reader, usher, musician)
(*LI*, 7), and urged what amounted to common sense: proper use of vestments, music that is not too loud, and so on. It also assured the faithful
that "desacralization" was in no way to be seen as part of the liturgical
reform. A sense of the sacred should always prevail in the rites of the
church. These three instructions on the implementation of the constitution followed one another in close succession. The next two would
not appear until much later, by authorization of Pope John Paul II:
Varietates Legitimae (1994), and *Liturgiam Authenticam* (2001).

**Five Instructions on the Implementation
of the Constitution on the Sacred Liturgy**

1964 Inter Oecumenici
First Instruction for the Right Implementation of the
Constitution on the Sacred Liturgy of the Second Vatican
Council

1967 Tres Abhinc Annos
Second Instruction for the Orderly Implementation of the
Constitution on the Liturgy of the Second Vatican Council

1970 Liturgicae Instaurationes
Third Instruction for the Orderly Implementation of the Constitution on the Sacred Liturgy of the Second Vatican Council

1994 Varietates Legitimae
Fourth Instruction for the Right Implementation of the
Constitution on the Sacred Liturgy of the Second Vatican
Council: Inculturation and the Roman Liturgy

2001 Liturgiam Authenticam
Fifth Instruction for the Right Implementation of the
Constitution on the Sacred Liturgy of the Second Vatican
Council: On the Use of Vernacular Languages in the Publication
of the Books of the Roman Liturgy

Those who lived through the initial changes flowing from Vatican
II remember it as both an exciting and a tumultuous time. A new vision
of liturgy was unfolding. In this era, many Catholics were studying the
Bible for the first time too, and thus could listen to the expanded readings at Mass with better understanding. In the celebration of the
Eucharist, they felt closer to the action, hence to Christ himself, as they
heard the words of institution spoken in their native tongue and could
see what the priest was doing.

For some, the passing away of the mystique of the old liturgy meant
the loss of a sense of mystery. Simplification resulted in banality—as if

one had pulled aside the curtain and found that the Wizard of Oz was really just a little man after all. For others, a new vitality was discovered in the liturgy. Passion for justice and peace, human rights, and solidarity seemed able to find an expression in the liturgy as it had not in the past, because Mass now included such things as the prayer of the faithful, new music replete with contemporary themes, and an exchange of the sign of peace with one's neighbors. For them, the sense of the sacred did not disappear, but rather was expanded to include the pressing concerns of human life in the present day.

Undoubtedly, some poor decisions were made in an excess of enthusiasm during this time. After so many centuries of stagnation, suddenly it seemed as if "anything goes." Some worthy artworks and music repertoire were imprudently tossed out, simply out of a preference for new things. The liturgy seemed at times like a canvas on which all kinds of concerns could be painted; thus there was a proliferation of different "kinds" of Masses: children's Masses, folk Masses, traditional Masses, organ Masses, clown Masses, youth Masses, charismatic Masses, and so on. Some liturgical changes were made without adequate explanation to the people, and a certain distress and confusion resulted even when parishioners were open to the "new" liturgy, because it interfered with lifelong habits and devotions. Change is never easy.

Catholics (both clergy and lay) tried to assimilate quickly ritual changes that would actually take generations for the church to fully inhabit, own, and realize at a deep spiritual level. At times, the clergy did not explain the changes well to the laity simply because they did not fully understand them. Even when the outward forms were followed in good faith and used with prudence, a suitable inner piety would take a long time to grow into the shape of its new liturgical expression.

Additional tensions were perhaps inevitable if only because the first implementation of the constitution was carried out in the 1960s, a time of crisis. Widespread social change and revolt against authority was peaking. Protests, some violent, were roiling society; acts of conscience and reports of bloodshed were in the news every day. The sexual revolution, the civil rights movement, and the women's movement were changing attitudes at a startling pace. Historians would look back at the 1960s as a watershed in the twentieth century. It is not surprising that the church should have experienced tumult during such a time, when civil society was embroiled in what amounted to a revolution. The liturgical reform was not a product of the 1960s. But the reactions to its implementation were very much influenced by the times.

Cultural anthropologist Gerald Arbuckle, SM, describes the 1960s as a "revolution of expressive disorder" marking the end of the modern period and the beginning of postmodernism.[5] Although the 1960s may seem like a long time ago, its aftermath can be felt even today. Reactions to the 1960s "revolution" can be grouped into "anti-order" and "pro-order" expressions, Arbuckle argues. On one hand, disillusionment with modernity and its assumptions, a fluid sense of self, and rejection of the founding myths of society flourish on the postmodern side. In opposition, the "pro-order" or "new right" has produced vigorous authoritarianism, fundamentalism, and a restorationist agenda.

To return to the liturgical reform centered in Rome, it is clear that the journey of the Consilium itself was not without its own upsets. Near the end of this period (1964–1970), a secret informant persuaded Pope Paul VI that the Consilium was claiming too much power for itself. The pope charged the organization with disloyalty, and a shake-up followed. In a short time, he set up a new agency as part of his reorganization of the Curia: the Congregation for Divine Worship. This body was created by splitting the Congregation of Rites in two. Henceforth, the newly reconfigured Congregation for Divine Worship was to work on liturgical issues. The task of completing the liturgical reform was handed over to them. Some members of the Consilium continued their service in specific task groups, but they now operated under the aegis of the Congregation for Divine Worship. The other part of what had been the Congregation of Rites became the Congregation for the Causes of Saints and was responsible solely for canonizations.

Cardinal Benno Gut, who headed the Consilium at the time of this transition, was put in charge of the Congregation for Divine Worship. The secretary for the Consilium, Archbishop Bugnini, was appointed its secretary. Continuity with the work of the Consilium was supported by this arrangement. But the method for carrying out the work in this body was the curial one, that is, it was highly formalized and inflexible. Study groups among the consultors continued, but the members of the congregation themselves were never able to discuss measures with a breadth of expertise present at the table. They ruled on what was presented. It was in this congregation that Archbishop Karol Wotyla, who later would become Pope John Paul II, served.

The work of liturgical reform was also occurring in places other than Rome. Local initiatives were many, and they were pursued vigorously. Rome responded, managed, and directed. Specific plans for inculturation of the liturgy arose at once, and new ones kept coming. These included adaptations such as the Thai "kiss of peace" with hands joined and touched to the forehead, the use of dance in Zaire (later renamed the Congo), the practice in Laos of having the celebrant sit while presiding at the Eucharist, dialogue homilies in Zambia, and the more frequent use of incense and, at times, perfumed water in Pakistan.[6] Communion under both forms was implemented only gradually, but the question of communion in the hand came to the surface very soon. Together these two developments created a very striking difference in the communion rite. Requests came in for new liturgical texts from Rome too, such as Eucharistic Prayers for Masses with children.

The revision of the Mass was implemented in such a way that the effects of the changes in the Eucharist were felt by everyone within a relatively short period of time. Although some may have dragged their heels, for the most part there was no "opting out" or long delay permitted in instituting the revised liturgy of the Mass. Some of the liturgical rites to emerge during the later stages of the reform, however, did so only slowly, and some reforms were never implemented in full.

The reformed *Rite of Penance*, for example, was released very late, in 1974, and experienced relatively weak implementation. The most striking innovation it contained, the provision for general absolution (Form Three), was almost immediately withdrawn in practice and reserved to situations so rare as to be practically nonexistent. Form Two, the communal service with individual confessions, was seldom used more than once or twice a year in most parishes,[7] and some never used it at all, or truncated it. Appendix II, which contains penitential services without the sacrament, is almost completely unknown to this day, even among the clergy. The renewed aspects of individual confession (Form One), such as use of scripture, were not promoted and thus frequently ignored. It is still common to find Catholics who begin their confession with the words "Bless me, Father, for I have sinned"—a formula not found in the new rite—and the concluding dialogue that ends the rite of individual reconciliation is almost completely unknown by the faithful. Finally, although there were some calls for developing a restored Order of

Penitents in the 1980s, they have not succeeded in creating much response.

Although prelates lament the decline in popular use of the sacrament, it is hardly surprising, given the fact that almost every element of renewal in that area has been suppressed, ignored, or given a lukewarm reception. Probably the most noted change in reconciliation took place simply by the omission of the requirement that priest and penitent be separated by a grille. Thus "face-to-face" confession, a very old tradition, came back into popular use. In such cases, the extension of the priest's hand over the head of the penitent is visible, and thus was restored as a noticeable liturgical sign of the sacrament. Yet reaction against the practice of face-to-face confession was also very quick, and in many places grilles remained or were re-installed.

On the other hand, the *Rite of Christian Initiation of Adults* (*RCIA*), released in 1972 and affectionately known as a "sleeper," has steadily increased in influence after an extremely poor start. Originally imagined as an initiation process for use in mission lands and in de-Christianized Europe, the rite has had its greatest implementation—surprisingly—in North America. Yet even in the United States, before the American bishops issued a text with local adaptations in 1988, few parishes touched it. Long, complex, and demanding, the rite was not considered "user friendly." Between 1988 and 2000, however, implementation of the rite skyrocketed to 75 percent of U.S. parishes, and the results have been very encouraging. The vast majority of American bishops surveyed for a study released in 2000[8] affirmed that the *Rite of Christian Initiation of Adults*, rightly implemented, "has the power to revitalize parish life." This stunning claim has no equal among the Vatican II reforms of the liturgy.

All this is to say that although many revised ritual books appeared within ten years of the council, the time frame for assessing the progress of these reforms varies considerably. Each of them has, in a certain sense, a life of its own, and while they all contribute to the greater picture, each follows its own trajectory, depending upon resources, needs, local leadership, and a host of other variables. Could the reform of penance yet prove to be a vibrant force for renewal in the church? Might the reformed Liturgy of the Hours, released in 1971, yet have a palpable influence on the daily spiritual life of the faithful? The prospect for such developments does not look good right now, but things can certainly change.

Meanwhile, back at the Vatican, again apparently catalyzed by secret denunciations, another reorganization of the agencies responsible for the liturgical reform took place in 1975. The Congregation for Divine Worship, which earlier had inherited the work of the Consilium, was subsumed under the Congregation for Sacraments. The secretary of the Congregation for Divine Worship, Archbishop Bugnini, who had served under three presidents of the congregation and played a crucial organizational role throughout the earlier stages of the reform since the time of Pope Pius XII, was removed from his position in Rome and assigned to a post in Iran.

This shift in personnel and organization was too sudden and dramatic to go unnoticed. What were the issues or motivations at work here? What was at stake? Personalities, politics, matters of principle? Bugnini recounts a political intrigue in the Vatican at that time, in which a secret dossier had been assembled and presented to the pope accusing him of being a freemason, a charge he absolutely denied. At the time, a vicious right-wing publication in Italy, *Si, Si, No, No*, fueled the conspiracy theory and added new names to the list of supposed freemasons, until 114 prelates stood accused. The Vatican did not respond to these accusations initially; their denial came quite late. Perhaps it perceived the charges as too ludicrous to merit a response. Could they have been taken seriously? No clear answers are available.

One thing can be said with certainty, however: the fact that there was no swift refutation from above opened the door to conjecture from below. By the time these events occurred, the liturgical reform was being used in the popular press as a scapegoat for a decline in Mass attendance and in vocations to the priesthood and religious life after the council. These "facts," added to the dissolution of the Congregation for Divine Worship, were cited by critics of the reform in the decades following as circumstantial evidence that the reform itself had fallen from favor.

With the departure of Bugnini and the closing of the Congregation for Divine Worship, an era was ending in Rome during which most of the creative work on the liturgy had taken place. It seemed that the liturgical reform had reached a plateau. The church had new books, guidelines, and directives, and now had to settle down to follow them and work out their implications. Pope John Paul II, elected in 1978, pledged to follow in the footsteps of his predecessors, Pope John XXIII and Pope Paul VI, in their commitment to Vatican II.

DEEPENING OF THE REFORM: 1975–1984

The period that followed the creative and tumultuous years of first implementation of the reforms was a time of growth in ownership and understanding of the new liturgy by the church at large. In the United States, the late 1970s and early 1980s were boom times for lay ministry training, and educational programs and institutions relating to liturgy flourished. Organizations such as the National Association of Pastoral Musicians (NPM) and the Federation of Diocesan Liturgical Commissions (FDLC) grew in size and influence, and academic programs in liturgy attracted many students. Some of the euphoria that accompanied the initial liturgical changes had worn off, but energy and interest in the liturgical renewal were still high. Better educated liturgists were staffing diocesan worship offices. There was less talk of experimentation and more of raising the quality and integrity of art, music, and ritual action in the liturgy. There were fewer "designer" Masses for diverse groups and there was more attention to worship as a unifying experience. There was less concentration on how we shape the liturgy and more concentration on how the liturgy shapes us.

How much did the worldwide church follow through on the constitution's mandate for liturgical education and formation in seminaries and religious houses (*SC*, 16)? If the situation in the United States is indicative, liturgical education in the seminaries during this period had not met the standard set by the constitution. A 1974 study by the Center for Applied Research in the Apostolate at Georgetown University showed that out of forty-five respondents (a 74 percent response rate), twenty-seven[9] (60 percent) reported that liturgy was not considered a major course of study in their curriculum. According to the study, 62 percent of the faculty who taught liturgy courses in seminaries did so only part-time. In addition, education in preaching, music, and the arts was poor. The study concludes that

> . . . the central problem of liturgy in the seminary curriculum is that of *its status*. In most seminaries, the optimum position given the study of liturgy is at best that of an ancillary discipline; more often it is merely that of a subdivision of sacramental theology. While many seminaries have faculty members who are competent to teach in the area of liturgical studies, it

is perhaps symptomatic of the *ancillary status of liturgy* that few seminaries have even one full-time person with an advanced degree in liturgical studies.[10]

In 1979, in response to worldwide requests, the Congregation for Catholic Education issued an Instruction on Liturgical Formation in Seminaries.[11] In addition to a number of paragraphs dealing with liturgical formation, celebration, and the practice of piety, this instruction includes in an appendix a detailed list of things to be taught. The instruction did not say anything new, but its appearance suggested that seminary education and formation in liturgy was a project "under construction" in many places around the globe, even by the late 1970s. In 1980, Nathan Mitchell reported that the situation in the United States had improved somewhat, though it still fell short of the council's directives.[12]

The one really novel development during this period was the rise of a brand new set of critical questions concerning the language of worship. New sensitivities to language began to develop in the 1970s among more educated, socially progressive Americans and some Europeans, following currents of thought that first arose in secular intellectual circles and in the academy. Feminists began to champion inclusive language and feminine or gender-neutral images of God, as well as the inclusion of women in all liturgical ministries. It was out of concern for inclusive language that the words of the Eucharistic Prayer concerning the Blood of Christ were changed in the mid-seventies from "It will be shed for you and for all men..." to "It will be shed for you and for all...." Other advocates called for the abandonment of militaristic metaphors, dominance/subjection imagery, and expressions thought to be racially pejorative or offensive to particular groups. In church settings, these were seen as moral issues. People began to "watch their language" for what it said, intentionally or unintentionally, about power relations and the assumptions of a moral universe in which violence and the subjugation of women and minorities were taken for granted. No longer was Latin versus the vernacular the key language issue. Liturgical language instead became a proving ground for moral arguments about gender equality, social justice, and peace.

Overall, however, the decade following 1975 was a period of stabilization rather than a period of unrest. In 1975, the North American Academy of Liturgy, established in 1973, began to hold annual meetings. Although a number of publishing endeavors devoted to the liturgy had been in place well before the council (the Liturgical Press in the United States was notable among them), new ones were added. For example, the Archdiocese of Chicago in 1977 founded a publishing house, Liturgy Training Publications, which has produced valuable resources for use at the parish level. Catechesis about the liturgy was improving. As Archbishop Rembert Weakland, OSB, of Milwaukee, observed, "The essentials of good liturgy were being emphasized and the needed sense of the sacred was being reestablished."[13] Some of the fruit of this time was ripening within Weakland's own archdiocese, where a ten-year consultation with composers of church music was under way under the leadership of Sister Theophane Hytrek, and would issue the "Milwaukee Statement" in 1991. After a period of much change, it was a time of settling and deepening.

This atmosphere was not limited to the United States. Cardinal Joseph Cordeiro, archbishop of Karachi and president of the Pakistan Episcopal Conference, in reflecting on the twentieth anniversary of *Sacrosanctum Concilium*, opined that the liturgical "revolution" of Vatican II had been accepted. In order to characterize the times, he contrasted the pre-conciliar situation with that after the Second Vatican Council. He described the church that had produced the reforms of Trent as a church that "lived in a state of siege":

> This state of tension and insecurity and the concern to "hold on" is reflected in the worship of the time: the clinging to Latin (which fewer and fewer people understood), the stress on centralizing (the priest and the altar boy made the Mass; the people came in almost as a kind of after-thought to "hear" the Mass), the vast distance and separation between the aisle and the sanctuary; the worship of a church in tension.

Twenty years after the council, he surveyed a very different situation: "... the Church not merely at worship, but *relaxing* at worship, relaxing to be herself as church, regardless of all else."[14] This atmosphere was soon to change, however.

CONFLICT AND CONTINUITY: 1984–2005

The turning point came in 1984, when Pope John Paul II granted permission for ongoing use of the liturgy that pre-dated the council. Commonly referred to as the Tridentine Mass, it is actually the 1962 edition of the Mass that is permitted. This edition includes the reforms of Pope Pius XII and Pope John XXIII that occurred before the council. The 1962 "Tridentine Mass" is to be distinguished from the Latin-language version of the "Novus Ordo," which is the liturgy produced after Vatican II. Although both may be celebrated in Latin, they are quite different from each other.

Permission for the Tridentine usage was later strengthened and given greater protection in 1988 with the establishment of the *Ecclesia Dei* Commission—ostensibly to reconcile those followers of Archbishop Marcel Lefèbvre who wanted to remain in communion with the Catholic Church after Lefèbvre's excommunication that same year.

Pope John Paul II had consulted with the world's bishops about his initial decision of 1984. They were almost unanimously opposed to it. Nevertheless, with the support of the Congregation for the Doctrine of the Faith, the pope decided to grant the indult. (The subsequent extension in 1988 was made without consultation.) The decision was to prove damaging to the development of a more mature stage of liturgical renewal. In the words of Rembert Weakland, archbishop of Milwaukee:

> Just at the moment when the situation was beginning to settle down and the deeper and more spiritual aspects of the renewal were becoming possible, a whole new battle began, one in which the renewal itself was brought into question or where everyone seemed free to project his or her personal views on how the renewal of the council should have taken place. As well-meaning as the decision to broaden the Tridentine usage was, one cannot emphasize enough how devastating the results have been. Not only was the liturgical renewal of the council called into question; the impression was created that, with sufficient protest, the whole of Vatican Council II could be reversed.[15]

Weakland wrote this in 1997. He was speaking in hindsight, after having seen a promising situation disintegrate. Certainly by the end of the 1990s in the United States the word "battleground" could be used to describe the liturgical scene. Liturgy was not the only scene of battle, to be sure. Polarization within the church on a whole range of issues throughout this time became so severe that it prompted Cardinal Joseph Bernardin of Chicago to launch in 1996 the "Common Ground Initiative," a forum for intra-ecclesial dialogue. But liturgy was certainly a prominent area of conflict.

Two stories illustrate the contentious climate of the liturgical scene in the 1990s: the ICEL revision of the Sacramentary, and the revision of the American Lectionary conducted by the U.S. Bishops' Committee on the Liturgy. They are worth looking at in detail, because they have had a definite impact on the implementation of the constitution. Yet they are not the whole picture. We will look also at other developments that took place during this time, developments that have been neither contentious nor attention-getting but simply part of the ongoing liturgical renewal launched by Vatican II.

In 1981, ICEL began a review and revision of the English translation of books that had been in circulation since the early seventies. This was not surprising. In the interim period, new editions had been produced in Rome. There was also a general desire to improve the English translations in light of the experience of using them. Some bishops continued to favor the spare and direct style of the first translations, while others called for revisions that would display greater richness of language and correspond more closely to the Latin. The move toward improvement and deepening reflection was characteristic of this time, and not the result of any particular crisis.

This massive project began with the revision of the 1969 funeral rite. The revised ICEL text was issued in 1985 as the *Order of Christian Funerals*. The revision of the 1973 ICEL edition of the Sacramentary had begun in 1982, with an extensive consultation of all the member episcopal conferences, their individual bishops, and the liturgical commissions of their countries and dioceses. Booklets of drafts were widely circulated. In the words of John Page, the American who was then executive secretary for ICEL, the first consultation yielded a mandate to proceed along the lines of developing a translation that would use "language that was indeed meant for public proclamation but that was also noticeably different from everyday speech, a language that was formal yet clear, majestic but not mannered, prayerful but not ritualistic."[16]

Both the first and the second stages of the consultation, in 1982 and 1986 respectively, garnered a small but very positive response from bishops and liturgical commissions across the conferences. The work continued smoothly and rather quietly, incorporating criticisms and making improvements. ICEL's efforts were in fact producing a more literal translation, with greater richness and fidelity to the Latin, but without the sacrifice of native idiom or intelligibility.

At the appearance of the third Progress Report however, in 1992, furious opposition to the project emerged. This was especially true in the United States, where small, vocal groups had in the interim found they could wield influence quite out of proportion to their size by the use of lobbying and tactics of intimidation. They had already intervened in the case of the American translation of the *Catechism*, and succeeded in having inclusive language removed from it. Now their sights were set even higher. The British publication, *The Tablet*, described these groups as follows:

> The often vituperative attacks have been led by conservative groups, especially in the United States. Fr Joseph Fessio's Ignatius Press, Mother Angelica's EWTN network, and publications such as *The Wanderer* and *Adoremus*, have, over the years identified John Page and ICEL as symbol of everything they loathe—feminism, modernism, and inculturation. Crusaders are urged to "police" liturgies in search of aberrations, and to notify Vatican personnel who ask bishops to look into the complaints. These groups, some of which are opposed to the vernacular Mass, often have the ear of high-ranking Vatican officials.[17]

In a characteristically judicious assessment, John Page himself described the campaign as follows:

> Groups were founded in the United States to convince the bishops that the Sacramentary revision was deeply flawed. Letter-writing campaigns to bring the work to a halt were aimed at the bishops and the Roman dicasteries. While certain points made by the critics were useful and had a positive influence within ICEL . . . the overall effect was regrettable. Many of the considerable improvements represented by the revision

over the 1973 texts were either unfairly caricatured or simply ignored. The debate chiefly centered on a few issues, inclusive language large among them. Unfortunately this atmosphere of harsh polemic would continue throughout the subsequent stages of the revision process and beyond.[18]

The attacks on the Sacramentary project proved successful. The revised Sacramentary, by then completed after fifteen years of intensive collaboration within the English-speaking Catholic community and formally approved by the canonical vote of the bishops' conferences throughout the world, was summarily scrapped by Rome. At Rome's insistence, the bishops of the board of ICEL were forced to draw up a new constitution for the commission that established it at the behest of the Holy See with the collaboration of the conferences of bishops, rather than as a joint commission erected at the behest of the confer-ences themselves, as it had been for forty years. By 2002, John Page was forced to retire. A Vatican committee, Vox Clara, was established, headed by Cardinal George Pell of Sydney, to oversee the progress of the English translation and to speed things up. The reconstituted ICEL immediately began a new translation of the Sacramentary (now to be called the Roman Missal). It was not until June of 2006, however, that the U.S. bishops' conference approved the first piece of that work, a new version of the Order of Mass. The bishops rejected several succes-sive drafts before the USCCB became the fourth conference to approve the text. They also approved a large number of amendments.

The new translation has been guided by an instruction prepared by the Congregation for Divine Worship and the Sacraments and pub-lished in 2001 with the approval of Pope John Paul II: *Liturgiam Authenticam*. This document unveiled a set of expectations regarding translations far different from the working principles followed in the past. In place of dynamic equivalence, which had been the philosophy applied in the 1969 Roman document *Comme le prévoit*, it asks for for-mal equivalence, that is, a more literal translation in which every Latin word must be accounted for. Faithfulness to the Latin is the overriding concern, with unity and doctrinal orthodoxy presumed to be the out-come of exactitude in translation. Original prayer compositions, such as those that had appeared in the Sacramentaries of many lands (the Italian Sacramentary is especially noteworthy in this regard) are now limited by so many conditions that it is difficult to imagine a situation in which new prayer texts would be deemed acceptable.[19]

The instruction is wide ranging, but it also pays close attention to inclusive language. In setting the groundwork, it makes these general assertions: lack of intelligibility is not by itself a problem (no. 27), and the task of avoiding the appearance of fostering injustice rests with the homilist and catechist, not the translator (no. 29). A pendulum swing away from *Sacrosanctum Concilium*'s call for clarity and intelligibility, in which liturgical texts "should normally not need much explanation," is in evidence here. Inclusive language itself is addressed in detail in paragraphs 30 and 31, which contain no fewer than seven subheadings, including such minutiae as the use of singulars and plurals, and what pronoun should be used for the church.

The instruction voices an admirable desire to have texts translated in a way that fully represents their richness and can withstand the test of time. Despite this positive content, however, it must on the whole be considered a very defensive document. Academic style manuals are not to be regarded as standards (no. 32). Similarities to non-Catholic translations are to be avoided, as "confusing" to the faithful (no. 40). Anxieties about doctrine abound in the text. The instruction even suggests that catechetical formulae, devotional prayers, and authorized translations of the *Catechism* be used to guide the translation of liturgical texts in certain instances (see no. 40 and no. 50a and b). This is a highly unusual proceeding, turning traditional ways of thinking around. Liturgy is normally considered "*theologia prima*" and therefore one of the *sources* for such theological reflection as a catechism or popular devotion might contain, rather than something modeled upon the wording of a catechism or devotion.

Although human language is always adapted to its context, *Liturgiam Authenticam* takes the view that liturgical language should remain a world apart. According to the document, this is because the words spoken in liturgy "express truths that transcend the limits of time and space" rather than "the interior dispositions of the faithful" (no. 19). The instruction aims at creating a "sacral" language in the vernacular (no. 47) that will correspond exactly to the Latin original. The arguments (unity, theological precision) are very similar to those that were advanced on behalf of Latin at the time of the council. In contrast to *Sacrosanctum Concilium*'s nuanced demand that the "substantial unity" of the Roman rite always be safeguarded, *Liturgiam Authenticam* directs that "[i]n preparing all translations of the liturgical books, the greatest care is to be taken to maintain the *identity and unitary expression* of the Roman rite" (no. 5; emphasis added). All the rubrics, titles, arrangements of texts, and the praenotanda (notes in the text) are to follow the Latin order, and not be rearranged (no. 69). Even the capitalization found in the Latin must be reproduced as much as possible (no. 33).

The instruction goes on to say that the "unitary expression" of the Roman rite is "a manifestation of the theological realities of ecclesial communion and unity" (no. 5). Communion (in Latin *communio*, in Greek *koinonia*) is a theological term that currently enjoys a high profile in church circles, both in the Catholic Church and in ecumenical discussion. By using it here, the instruction seems to be assigning considerable theological weight to its demands. Communion and unity are no small matters. In fact, the Extraordinary Synod of Bishops in 1985 asserted that communion was the crucial category voiced by Vatican II for understanding the church itself. The Congregation for the Doctrine of the Faith in 1992 affirmed that "the concept of communion (*koinonia*)...is very suitable for expressing the core mystery of the church..."[20] If unitary expression—all the way down to identical arrangement of notes and so forth—is needed to express unity and communion, it must be very important.

One cannot help but wonder, however, whether the instruction is putting more weight on the details of translation than they can reasonably be expected to bear. No move has been made to remove the indult for use of the Tridentine Mass (surely *the* major departure from the idea of a "unitary expression" of the Roman rite); and the instruction fully supports the provisions on inculturation stated by *Varietates Legitimae*, which may result in many differences in how the liturgy is celebrated. If literal translation of texts is a necessity in service to ecclesial communion, it would seem that widely divergent liturgical expressions cannot be tolerated at the same time; and yet they are.

The document allows cooperation with non-Catholic groups in the preparation of texts, provided that such groups are large communities and are represented by persons who enjoy a genuine role of authority in those communities (no. 91). But by suggesting that similarities to texts used by other ecclesial communities is a problem (no. 40), the document calls into question the purpose of such cooperation. Indeed,

Catholic participation in a number of ecumenical organizations devoted to liturgical texts was withdrawn upon publication of the document. Horace T. Allen, Jr., professor of worship at Boston University School of Theology and founding co-chair of the English Language Liturgical Consultation (the ELLC succeeded ICET in 1984 as the coordinating body for international ecumenical work on common texts) said in an address to the Centro Pro Unione in Rome after the issuance of the document: "I will simply now report to you from North America and the English-speaking world that the entire liturgical and ecumenical conversation are gone. Finished. Done."[21] While this is almost certainly an overstatement, it is one that illustrates the immediate impact of the instruction on dialogue partners who had enjoyed a long history of Catholic cooperation prior to this instruction.

Liturgiam Authenticam is presented as the fifth instruction on the right implementation of *Sacrosanctum Concilium*. Yet it is difficult, if not impossible, to reconcile the insular and defensive aspects of the instruction with *Sacrosanctum Concilium*'s concerns for ecumenism, inculturation, clarity, and intelligibility, as well as the practical use of relevant expertise in service to the liturgy. The instruction has been extremely unpopular, not only in the English-speaking world, but throughout Europe. How could it be otherwise? It asserts that the "right" implementation of the council's document is, in many respects, to do the exact opposite of what has been done for the past forty years.

It is important to note that as the Catholic Church has continued on the path of ecumenism, its willingness to affirm a variety of liturgical expressions *outside* the Roman rite has indeed broadened. For example, the same year that *Liturgiam Authenticam* (with its insistence upon keeping Latin syntax and capitalization patterns in the Roman rite) was released, the Catholic Church entered into a historic agreement with the Assyrian Church of the East. In this agreement, the Catholic Church acknowledged the validity of the Anaphora of Addai and Mari, which has served as the Assyrian church's Eucharistic Prayer from ancient times.[22] This anaphora has no institution narrative. That is to say, it does not tell the story of the Last Supper. Put in blunt terms, the text that most Catholics would call "the consecration" is not, and has never been present in the Anaphora of Addai and Mari. The whole of the prayer, in a way quite different from the Roman rite, consecrates the elements. The Catholic Church today, for good and just reasons, now officially considers this Eucharist valid. Thus, at the dawn of the new millennium, one sees a push from Rome toward literalism and away from ecumenical work on texts within the Roman rite, expressed in *Liturgiam Authenticam*. But at the same time one sees that in other official acts of the Catholic Church, in service to ecumenism, some very different ways of approaching liturgical texts are manifest.

In the disputes over language within the Roman rite, all parties acknowledge that the English translation is an important one for the worldwide church, because English is now the *lingua franca* of our times. What Latin once was for the Roman Empire, English is today for the worldwide church. Many of the smaller language groups, in fact, use English translations as a point of reference when making their own translations. The Vatican has therefore been watching the journey of the new Sacramentary closely, and we may plausibly consider the progress or failure of the project in English as a test case for the world.

The first three drafts of ICEL's new translation of the Order of Mass section of the Sacramentary (now called the Roman Missal) were not found acceptable by the American bishops. Many deemed them stilted and archaic, difficult both to speak and to understand. The bishops of England and Wales also criticized the work of the new translation for its "lengthy sentences, poor syntax and archaic language."[23] Although usually extremely docile toward directives from Rome, the American bishops were reluctant to approve a translation that could prove to be a pastoral nightmare—unused and unusable. As Cardinal Roger M. Mahoney, archbishop of Los Angeles observed after the first unsuccessful draft, "We simply cannot have a translation that is labored and is not easily proclaimed or understood. . . . Following the [clerical sex abuse] scandal, the last thing our people need is to now disrupt the liturgy, which has been a source of nourishment and strength during this difficult journey."[24]

The story of the revised American Lectionary is disheartening in some similar ways. The first edition of the Lectionary for Mass had been produced in 1969. In 1981, the Congregation for Divine Worship and the Discipline of the Sacraments issued the second edition of the lectionary, which was routine business. The U.S. Bishops' Committee on the Liturgy was commissioned by the bishops to oversee a new translation into English of the scripture texts for the lectionary. The translation was completed in 1992 and endorsed by more than the two-thirds majority of the bishops which is required. Concerning the first volume, 219 bishops voted in favor of it; 27 were opposed. The Congregation for Divine Worship and the Discipline of the Sacraments, however, did not confirm it.

Some additional background on inclusive language will help to make sense of the collision that took place. As was mentioned earlier, concerns about gender inclusive language had arisen in the 1970s and early 1980s. By the end of the 1980s, churches had been struggling with these questions for some time. The bishops of North America addressed the issue publicly, in a moderate fashion. The bishops' conference of Canada spoke to the question sympathetically in 1989 ("To Speak as a Christian Community: Pastoral Message on Inclusive Language") and in 1990 the U.S. Conference of Catholic Bishops offered pastoral guidelines that charted a moderate course ("Criteria for the Evaluation of Inclusive Language Translations of Scriptural Texts Proposed for Liturgical Use"), keeping traditional language for God and the Trinity but encouraging inclusive language when speaking of people, that is, "horizontal" inclusive language.

Why did the Vatican congregation refuse to confirm the new translation of the lectionary? The main reason for the rejection was, in the words of Bishop Donald Trautman of Erie, then chairman of the Bishops' Committee on the Liturgy: "A seeming connection was made between horizontal inclusive language and the question of the ordination of women. What began as an attempt to bring about inclusivity in accord with contemporary English usage now became a serious doctrinal matter."[25]

After the initial refusal to confirm the text, extended discussions about how to revise the English translation of the lectionary ensued from 1993 to 1996. For the American bishops, the question of women's ordination was quite separate from the issue of inclusive language. They spoke from within the perspective of their country, their culture, and their flock. But Rome was persistent in not taking their word for it.

In December 1996, all seven active cardinals in the United States went to Rome and met with the prefects of the Congregation for the Doctrine of the Faith and the Congregation for Divine Worship and the Discipline of the Sacraments, to move along the process of approval for the lectionary. An agreement was reached in which three American bishops would go to Rome on behalf of the bishops' conference and meet with representatives of these congregations and a translator. One of the conditions subsequently set by Rome was that none of the American bishops present could be a scripture scholar. The delegation was sent, and a substantially changed translation was produced in twelve days.

The bishops of the United States had reservations about the text produced. Quite apart from its lack of inclusive language, it seemed clumsy, hard to proclaim, and hard to understand. But they compromised by approving the text, with the stipulation that it be reviewed in five years. It was resubmitted to the Holy See. Four additional years passed before approval was given, finally, in 2001—the same year in which *Liturgiam Authenticam* appeared. Nine years were expended, all told, for what should have been a routine matter.

The idea that Rome is bound to treat with respect the judgment of the local bishops' conference on liturgical matters was certainly called into question by this bruising exchange. The affront was as keen in this instance as it was in the business of ICEL and the Sacramentary. Here too the subject was clearly within the competence of the bishops, in this case a single episcopal conference, but it was taken out of the bishops' hands. After having accepted all conditions, even those of questionable wisdom, they were made to wait an additional four years for the approval they sought.

As the stipulation of review implies, the issuance and use of the new translation has been followed by consultation. A survey of bishops and their staffs in 2003 has already shown widespread dissatisfaction with the text.

As these developments were under way, the implementation of the liturgical reforms of Vatican II nevertheless was proceeding on other fronts without great conflict. Very little of the insularity and defensiveness of *Liturgiam Authenticam* can be seen in the fourth instruction, *Varietates Legitimae*, on inculturation and the Roman liturgy, issued in 1994, for example. This document pertains specifically to articles 37–40 of *Sacrosanctum Concilium*. Although cautious in tone and concerned with a disciplinary agenda that has a centralizing focus, *Varietates Legitimae* carries through the principles found in the Constitution on the Sacred Liturgy.

Varietates Legitimae articulates a variety of sophisticated problems to be taken into account when inculturating the liturgy, and even reviews salvation history with respect to the subject of inculturation.

The situations it addresses include multi-cultural populations, challenges brought by immigration, the co-existence of traditional societies with more urban and industrial cultures, the potential problems of politicization of cultural symbols and the romanticizing of folkloric customs, and so on. It does not descend to minutiae or claim to have a formula to fit every circumstance. The instruction allows for a process of discernment to take place in the context of a dialogue that includes specialists (in the Roman rite and in the social sciences), pastors, and "wise people" from within each culture. *Sacrosanctum Concilium* had allowed for the possibility of a modest and, alternatively, a more profound inculturation of the liturgy. The instruction supports both options, and it outlines processes for achieving these ends.

Two observations about *Varietates Legitimae* will help to highlight certain developments it embodies in thinking about the Constitution on the Sacred Liturgy. First, it calls the translation of liturgical texts into vernacular languages "the first significant measure of inculturation" (no. 53). We saw earlier that the fathers of the council did not discuss the vernacular as a measure of inculturation, but rather viewed the shift from Latin into the vernacular under the aegis of "updating to the times."

The changeover to inculturation as the umbrella for use of the vernacular is completely taken for granted by *Varietates Legitimae*. The idea of "updating to the times" indeed is rarely mentioned anymore, and does not appear here. Rather, the timeless is sought. Through inculturation, the church seeks "the permanent values of a culture, rather than their transient expressions" (no. 5). The evolutionary and adaptive character of culture is never mentioned. If it were, of course further helpful discussion could follow.

Second, the expression "substantial unity of the Roman rite" had been used in *Sacrosanctum Concilium* to describe what must be preserved amidst diversity. Substantial unity was not defined. Some have suggested that the instruction *Varietates Legitimae* now has defined this concept by saying that substantial unity is expressed through the approved liturgical books—both the locally approved books and the Roman typical editions.[26] This assertion can mislead the unwary, however. The document never says *what* that unity is, only *where* it is expressed. Too much emphasis on the books themselves would be unfortunate, because it could portend a drift to "formal" unity, and a whole new exercise of literalism with respect to approved texts would logically follow. This may in fact be what was intended, with the literalism of *Liturgiam Authenticam* its logical outcome, but such an outcome is not explicated in *Varietates Legitimae*.

A careful look at Pope John Paul II's expression, and paragraph 36 of the document which expands it, shows that another interpretation is possible, and indeed likely. The books "express" substantial unity. The substance of unity still "stands beneath." It is something unseen, requiring outward forms to give it expression. This seems a healthier concept, honoring concrete forms (books) and requiring the church to care for them, but not equating the underlying unity of the Roman rite with such forms absolutely.

Of what does the substantial unity of the Roman rite consist, then? In an essay published in 2000, "Roman Genius Revisited," one of the elders of the liturgical renewal, Father Burkhard Neunheuser, OSB, of Maria Laach Abbey, offers a profound reflection. After discussing the history of Edmund Bishop's seminal essay, "The Genius of the Roman Rite," which was first delivered as a lecture in 1899, Neunheuser affirms Bishop's central insight: that the genius of the ancient Roman liturgy, preserved in all subsequent historical epochs even when its liturgical forms were greatly modified, can be summed up in two words: "soberness and sense." To this, however, he adds his own observation—that the theological elements proper to the liturgy are also constitutive of the Roman rite's unity, its genius.

> ... the developments of later times make us see that the genius of the old, original Roman Liturgy lies not only in its "soberness and sense," but also in the theological elements which underlie the Roman Liturgy. Actually, it was this fact among others which convinced the fathers of the Second Vatican Council to allow the reforms "provided that the fundamental unity of the Roman Rite is preserved" (*SC*, 38).... Again, we must ask, what are the essential features ("das Wesentliche") of the Roman Rite? In my article, I expressed it as follows: "Certainly, it is not the Latin language, nor the details of the Ordo Missae, nor the order of the Lectionary, the addition of a homily, the intercessions or other details. It is something much more important and fundamental." In interpreting what is essential, I pointed to the *Instructio "Inter Oecumenici"* of 26

September 1964, which states that it was not the intention of
the liturgical reform simply to change the forms and texts, but
to implement a pastoral practice the decisive power of which
"in eo posita est ut Mysterium Paschale vivendo exprimatur" [is
placed in it so that the Paschal Mystery may be expressed in
living[27]].[28]

Neunheuser goes on to name the theological elements that are always
present, and that were brought to clear focus by the council: the liturgy
is a sacred action which is the work of Christ and of his body the
church; it is the summit and source of Christian life and is the most outstanding of sacred actions; and, finally, the orientation of this worship
is to the Father, through the Son, and in the Holy Spirit.

Varietates Legitimae was produced in 1994. In 1998, Pope John Paul
II published an apostolic letter, *Dies Domini*, which was a beautiful and
rich reflection on Sunday. It occasioned no controversy at all. A flurry
of writings on the liturgy then appeared toward the end of the pope's
life. His apostolic letter on the fortieth anniversary of the Constitution
on the Sacred Liturgy, *Spiritus et Sponsa* (2003) was closely followed by
the encyclical *Ecclesia de Eucharistia* (2003). These did not prove contro-
versial either. His apostolic letter inaugurating the year of the
Eucharist, *Mane Nobiscum Domine*, released in October 2004, called
attention to the importance of well-celebrated liturgical signs and the
need for a profound mystagogical penetration of their meaning. In this
letter he also placed great emphasis on the consequences of liturgical
piety, such as church unity, human solidarity, social justice, and care for
the poor. Pope John Paul II viewed the path forward as one of continuity with the work following the council: "In the twentieth century, especially since the Council, there has been a great development in the way
the Christian community celebrates the sacraments, especially the
Eucharist. It is necessary to continue in this direction, and to stress particularly *the Sunday Eucharist* and *Sunday* itself…"[29]

In support of *Sacrosanctum Concilium* and of the reform of the
liturgy begun at Vatican II, the *Catechism of the Catholic Church* (1997)
and the *General Directory for Catechesis* (1997) exerted a positive influence. The *Catechism* is imbued with the thinking of *Sacrosanctum
Concilium* and supports catechesis on the liturgy at every level. The
General Directory makes special note of the problem of an inadequate

link between liturgy and catechesis in our time (*GDC*, 30), and it recommends liturgical catechesis as "a privileged means" of inculturating the faith (*GDC*, 207).

On the other hand, the revised General Instruction of the Roman Missal (2003) and the disciplinary document issued by the Congregation for Worship and the Discipline of the Sacraments, *Redemptionis Sacramentum* (2004), have occasioned some negative reactions. They fuss over details, sometimes at the expense of central signs and pastoral values. For example, communion under both forms is made more awkward and difficult by certain provisions. The congregation has offered no flexibility in addressing the obvious problems, however. It has suggested that if there are difficulties in following the new rules, communion from the cup should be omitted. Here one sees a regrettable development. The constitution offered a modest step in the direction of sharing the cup with the laity, but allowed permission for it to be extended depending on local conditions. Now, forty years later, in a legitimate development, many dioceses have embraced the practice and it has become dear to the people. For a curial congregation to take a hard-nosed attitude about the cup today, as if such development had never occurred, is bound to be viewed as restrictive and a step backwards.

A NEW REFORM?

A certain amount of confusion has been created by those who would like to see the liturgical reforms of Vatican II either reversed or redirected. One example of a misleading analysis, taken very seriously at the time, is the one advanced by Monsignor M. Francis Mannion in an article that appeared in *America* magazine in 1996.[30]

In this essay, the Irish-born monsignor, then rector of the cathedral of the Madeleine in Salt Lake City, Utah, describes no fewer than five separate "agendas for liturgical reform" at work concerning the liturgy at that time. According to Mannion, they are (1) advancing official reform, (2) restoring the preconciliar, (3) reforming the reform, (4) inculturating the reform, and (5) recatholicizing the reform.

He admits that the first agenda is so broad it is impossible to summarize. The last agenda belongs to Mannion himself, who organized like-minded individuals a few years earlier to compose the "Snowbird

Statement" concerning church music, and to found the Society for Catholic Liturgy. The name of his agenda, "recatholicizing the reform," seems to cast doubt on the catholicity of the reforms proceeding from authoritative sources. Mannion denies this, but it stands to reason that one cannot "recatholicize" something unless it has first been "decatholicized." Nevertheless, the "recatholicizing" agenda is not explicitly opposed to the reforms produced after council. It is devoted instead to promoting an elevated spirituality and high art forms, and to reinterpreting the council in terms favorable to these interests.

Mannion acknowledges some overlap between those who are interested in inculturation and those who advance the "official reform," but nonetheless separates the two agendas. This is so that he can include in the inculturation camp those who propose unauthorized innovations, such as some feminists, blacks, Hispanics, and other ethnic minorities, as well as those who are at home with "happy clappy" worship styles, and priests who conduct the liturgy as if they were game show hosts. This grouping thus confuses a number of issues, lumping together ideologues, special interest groups, and the ill-formed or merely ignorant, with thoughtful advocates, such as Father Anscar Chupungco, OSB, who deal responsibly with profound issues. In sum, separating out the agenda of "inculturation" from that of "official reform" supports a tendency to regard articles 37–40 of the constitution as a kind of Trojan horse. In fact, as we have seen, inculturation has been part and parcel of the official reform from the beginning, and was reinforced by *Varietates Legitimae* as recently as 1994.

This leaves two "agendas for reform" that are particularly interesting, not least because of how they are presented. The restorationists (agenda 2) and the advocates of "reform of the reform" (agenda 3) are treated with great courtesy, even deference. Mannion does not mention that some of the proponents of the restorationist trend—the followers of Archbishop Lefèbvre—are in schism, or that the movement tends to attract lunatics, such as the priest who attempted to assassinate Pope John Paul II in 1982 at Fatima and those who promote a form of traditionalism called "sedevacantism" (the belief that no pope after Pope Pius XII is legitimate). Still others in this movement are enmeshed in right-wing politics seeking the restoration of the monarchy in France, and others are embroiled in controversies over illegal occupation of churches in Paris. Mannion glosses over the absence of any scholarly support for restorationist claims by casting their movement as "popular," while confidently predicting that some solid scholarly work will come forth from them soon.

Those who would later read *The Problem of the Liturgical Reform*, produced by the Society of Saint Pius X in 2001, would be disappointed in this expectation. Much of the book's research amounts to careful documentation of the admirably consistent point of view exemplified by the *periti* of the council, the documents themselves, the *Catechism of the Catholic Church* and the writings of Pope John Paul II—a point of view which they reject. Archbishop Bernard Fellay, the current leader of the Society of Saint Pius X, tries to create the impression that differences over the Mass have always been the only real obstacle to unity for this schismatic group, which, of course, is also widely known for rejecting the council's teaching on ecumenism, religious freedom, collegiality of bishops, and the church in the modern world.

Joined with them in desiring a restoration of the pre-conciliar liturgy are the Catholics in union with Rome who currently take part in the 1962 or "Tridentine" Mass. How big is this group? In the United States, the article states, perhaps 15,000 to 20,000 attend such celebrations. Mannion augments his estimate of the numbers of traditionalists by guessing that there are sizable numbers of Catholics who would prefer the Tridentine Mass, but who go along with the Mass of Vatican II grudgingly.

Why does Mannion treat the restorationists as the bearers of an "agenda for reform" that needs to be present at the table? The answer may lie with the second most conservative group, who call for "reforming the reform." Mannion gives credit for the popularization of this expression to Monsignor Klaus Gamber of the liturgical institute of Regensburg, whose book *The Reform of the Roman Liturgy* appeared in English in 1993. A number of other writers say that (then Cardinal) Joseph Ratzinger coined it. Whatever the case, Ratzinger endorsed the French edition of Gamber's book. The book first appeared in German in 1984, the year that the indult was granted for the Tridentine Mass. There is no question that the work is highly sympathetic to the restorationist agenda. Gamber, however, thinks this crusade too important to be left to "a small group of fanatics" who reject the council outright.[31]

For Mannion's purposes, it is desirable to cast the "reform of the reform" group as moderates, quite separate from the restorationists. In fact, the restorationists have embraced Gamber as their own. The glow-ing preface to the English edition gives evidence of this. It was supplied by F. Gerard Calvet, OSB, the abbot of the monastery of St. Madeleine in France, which uses the Tridentine rite exclusively in its worship.

Gamber does not dismiss the liturgical movement leading up to the council, it is true. But he rejects with horror the reforms that followed the council:

> Great is the confusion! Who can still see clearly in this dark-ness? Where in our church are the leaders who can show us the right path? Where are the bishops courageous enough to cut out the cancerous growth of modernist theology that has implanted itself and is festering within the celebration of even the most sacred mysteries before the cancer spreads and causes even greater damage? ... We can only hope and pray that the Roman Church will return to Tradition and allow once more that liturgy of the Mass which is well over 1,000 years old.[32]

He claims, incredibly, that the reforms following the council have done "nothing"[33] to increase participation. What does he propose instead? Mannion leaves it vague, but Gamber himself is quite clear. He wants the Tridentine Mass. Only three changes in it seem to him to have been needed to bring about all the participation of the faithful envisioned by the council: the addition of one more reading, proclamation of the read-ings in the vernacular, and the introduction of the prayer of the faithful.[34] This, by any standard, is a rather meager harvest to reap from the exer-tions of an ecumenical council, but it seems sufficient to him. Gamber also expresses a definite view about the current Mass. He would like it to no longer be considered the Roman rite, but merely a rite *ad experimen-tum*, until it dies out.[35] Nevertheless, Mannion claims Gamber represents the agenda of a "much more moderate group" than the restorationists. Ratzinger himself opined that Gamber is "the one scholar who, among the army of pseudo-liturgists, truly represents the liturgical thinking of the center of the Church."[36] One may be forgiven for puzzling over how Gamber's thinking could be characterized as "much more moderate" or as representative of "the center of the Church." The only way that such an evaluation might appear justifiable is if the sedevacantists and Lefèbvrites loom very large on one's mental horizon.

As of 1988, the number of adherents to the Society of Saint Pius X was 150,000 people worldwide.[37] In that same year, there were 896,878,000 Catholics.[38] That would make the core restorationists equivalent to .0001672 percent of the Catholic community. If one doubles or even triples the number to include those reconciled through the 1984 indult or the Ecclesia Dei commission, this is still an incredibly small group.

Mannion notes the role of the American publicist, Father Joseph Fessio, SJ, in the "reform of the reform" agenda, but Fessio is more a promoter than a liturgical visionary. The two strategists in the "reform of the reform" camp whom Mannion mentions are the Australian co-founder of *Adoremus*, Father Brian Harrison, OS (now teaching theology in Puerto Rico), and Father Aidan Nichols, OP, the prolific British theologian. Neither claim any scholarly credentials in liturgical studies. They enter the discussion because, as Nichols says, "liturgy is too important to leave to the liturgists." According to Mannion's summary, Harrison wants women out of the sanctuary, fewer scripture readings, exclusive use of the old Roman canon in Latin, communion restricted to one form, and the priest's back to the people. These moves, we are expected to believe, are derived from the principles of *Sacrosanctum Concilium*. Nichols, in his book *Looking at the Liturgy* (1996), briefly flirts with the idea of promoting the Latin version of the Mass of Vatican II, with the priest's back to the people, but ultimately rejects such a course as a poor half-measure. In the end he recommends that the Tridentine Mass be re-instituted with a few minor revisions, and the Mass of Paul VI kept only for those communities that have grown attached to it. He notes that groups converting to Catholicism from the Episcopal or the Lutheran churches might wish to use it too, and that it could be used as "the basis for development of new ritual families" for Catholics in "young churches with indigenous cultures far removed from the Semitic-Graeco-Roman world of Bible and Fathers."[39] He cites India as "an obvious example" of the latter, but the suggestion seems somewhat less obvious when one recalls that the existence of Catholic Christianity in India may go back as far as the first century.

Mannion's article ends with a "cautionary note" to the custodians of the official reform. He warns them that if they do not take the other agendas more seriously, they will "suffer a massive loss of confidence at all levels of Catholic life." This ultimatum, delivered in 1996, when, as we have seen, self-appointed watchdogs were already successfully attacking liturgical projects by their direct appeals to Rome, sounded scary indeed. Mannion promises, however, that the official reform can avoid marginalization by being willing to "recognize more seriously the existence of the other agendas, to consider them sympathetically and not just critically and to moderate itself in view of their legitimate aims and ideals."

Why is it important that, to quote Mannion again, the "official agenda" take seriously such radical proposals and those who promote them, and "moderate itself in view of their legitimate aims"? Why did he judge their aims to be legitimate? The answer is, manifestly, not that they were popular, not that they were pastoral, not that they were moderate, not that they represented the center, not that their scholarship beat that of the periti at the council, not that they flowed from the principles of *Sacrosanctum Concilium*, but simply because influential cardinals favored them. Monsignor Mannion, it would appear, found out which way the wind was blowing in Rome.

If liturgy were only a matter of practical politics, the election of Cardinal Ratzinger as Pope Benedict XVI in 2005 should set the "reform of the reform" bandwagon groaning under the weight of new passengers. But in fact, the situation is not so simple. In the clear light of day, one begins to wonder if in fact the subscribers to *Adoremus*, the souls who pine for the Tridentine Mass, the advocates of some kind of radical "reform of the reform," and even the recatholicizers have not been estimated far beyond their actual value. Like shadow puppets, with a certain light behind them they can appear large and overwhelming in their influence. But are they really?

When, in 1989, Pope John Paul II reflected upon the implementation of the constitution twenty-five years after the council, he reported no widespread disaffection, no alarming decay. In his words: "The vast majority of the pastors and the Christian people have accepted the liturgical reform in a spirit of obedience and indeed joyful fervor."[40] He went on to acknowledge, citing the 1985 Extraordinary Synod of Bishops, that "[f]or many people the message of the Second Vatican Council has been experienced principally through the liturgical reform."[41] Had this been a disaster, calling for a complete revisioning from the ground up, one would think he would have mentioned it. But no, the problems he names are human faults rather than liturgical flaws: indifference, apathy, the desire of some to return to previous forms they consider a guarantee of orthodoxy, outlandish innovations, and departing from norms and authority. He addresses these problems as peripheral phenomena, not as the core or as the outgrowth of something fundamentally unsound. There is no mention of reforming the reform. In the opinion of Pope John Paul II, "The most urgent task is that of the biblical and liturgical formation of the people of God, both pastors and faithful."

Could Pope John Paul II and his legacy be part of Mannion's admonished "official reform" that is in danger of suffering "a massive loss of confidence at all levels"? Obviously, this would be a very embarrassing denouement. But let us consider the evidence. Pope John Paul II's contributions to the liturgy took place on a number of fronts. He might indeed be considered a significant shaper of the agenda of official reform. While still a bishop, he served in the Congregation for Divine Worship, and thus was instrumental in approving a great number of revised liturgical texts. During his pontificate, he produced the apostolic letter *Dies Domini*, On Keeping the Lord's Day Holy, which is a masterly work of teaching in the spirit of the new liturgy. Published in 1998, it is still far ahead of the majority of Catholics in its understanding of time and of the place of Eucharist in the rhythm of the week. His *Letter to Artists* (1999) lauds the constitution's "spirit of profound respect for beauty" and echoes its regard for the "noble ministry" of artists, while calling for a renewed dialogue between artists and the church.

On the fortieth anniversary of the Constitution on the Sacred Liturgy, Pope John Paul II still did not sound alarms or call for any rewriting of the reform. In *Spiritus et Sponsa* he advised: "...what is needed is a *pastoral care of the Liturgy* that is totally faithful to the new *ordines* [liturgical books]" (*SS*, 8). The future prospects for liturgical renewal he described were these: liturgy in service to the new evangelization, recovery of the art of mystagogic catechesis, appreciation for silence, developing a "taste for prayer" through broader use of the Liturgy of the Hours, and the exercise of pastoral guidance and discernment in following the norms of the church faithfully and creatively (*SS*, 11–15). His encyclical *Ecclesia de Eucharistia*, written near the end of his life (2003), is a passionate and personal reflection on the eucharistic mystery. Although he grieves over "abuses" in this rather ponderous work, he still emphatically affirms the reforms flowing from the council: "Certainly, *the liturgical reform inaugurated by the Council* has greatly contributed to a more conscious, active and fruitful participation in the Holy Sacrifice of the Altar on the part of the faithful."[42] He did not share Klaus Gamber's dysphoria. Even at this late date in Pope John Paul II's life, one glimpses the pontiff who was able to energize crowds of youth around the world, when one reads his exhortation to "Eucharistic amazement."

Under Pope John Paul II the revision of the liturgical books called for by the council was completed, with the release of the *Ceremonial of Bishops* and the *Book of Blessings* (both in 1989), and the new *Roman Martyrology* (2001, revised in 2004). He resisted the idea of women's ordination, but it was he who first admitted females to the role of altar server. The instruction on inculturation, discussed earlier, and the *Directory on Popular Piety and the Liturgy*, which firmly supports Vatican II principles concerning the liturgy, were both published during his pontificate. These are not groundbreaking, revolutionary works. They are oriented toward carrying out the implications of a reform well-founded at Vatican II, and implemented responsibly.

The only evidence one can show to support the idea that Pope John Paul II himself experienced disquiet over the way that the reform has been implemented after the council are the two disciplinary instructions issued near the end of his life by the Congregation for Divine Worship and the Discipline of the Sacraments: *Liturgiam Authenticam* and *Redemptionis Sacramentum*. Yet even these cannot really be used to advance the suggestion that the reform should begin all over again. After all, the liturgical books that are so zealously and literally defended by these two instructions are the ones produced following the council.

Weakland's observation about a change in climate "on the ground" remains valid. It is true that under the reign of Pope John Paul II reactionary individuals and groups got the green light, whether from policy decisions or "influential cardinals" or conservative episcopal appointments that took place for whatever reason. It was on Pope John Paul II's watch that paranoia about liturgical translations was given free reign, thus the untimely dumping of the ICEL Sacramentary translation, the American Lectionary debacle, and the issuance of the widely unpopular instruction *Liturgiam Authenticam*. And there is a certain nastiness, an "atmosphere of harsh polemic" that has clouded the issues, to the detriment of charity. Some are of the opinion that Pope John Paul II spent so much time traveling, writing, and speaking to the world that he had little left for attending to things like episcopal appointments and overseeing the Curia. Whatever the case, there have been wasteful setbacks, and a contentious atmosphere continues to absorb energy that might otherwise be used in service.

At the same time, it would be premature to judge the reform bankrupt, as *Adoremus* is wont to do, or to proclaim, as *National Catholic Reporter* columnist John Allen put it, that the conservatives have "won" the "liturgy wars."[43] A much more moderate assessment is warranted by the facts. Most pastors and parishes have embraced the reform. Most Catholics come to the liturgy not to "police" the "liberal establishment" or to fight a "liturgy war" but to pray. If those who have been in the vanguard of change should feel some disappointment that the reform hasn't yet produced more fruit,[44] this is only the natural result of the depths of human yearning that the project has activated. It is a stage on the way to more profound renewal.

PART IV

THE STATE OF THE QUESTIONS

During the question and answer period at the end of a recent talk on the Constitution on the Sacred Liturgy, a woman expressed puzzlement that we should be discussing the council as though its implementation were still going on. "Isn't Vatican II over?" she asked, "I thought we did all that." She was voicing a couple of popular assumptions. On the one hand, her confidence that the church "did all that" was an affirmation of the work that was done immediately after the council. On the other hand, her question suggested that the church has completed the work of Vatican II, and is (perhaps) ready to get on to something else.

Another point of view, in a quite different setting, was voiced by a young priest studying in Rome, who expressed the opinion that his generation is uniquely able to create a "synthesis" between Vatican II and what came before it. Vatican II, for him, was an influence to be judged and reconciled with previous eras, not—as the previous generation of priests would have known it—the framework for a future to which the church is wholly committed. In this view, Vatican II may not be over, but it is more like the swing of a pendulum, to be balanced by a new generation.

Are we finished with Vatican II? Is it time for a new synthesis? In a collection of interviews with thirty-three council participants and observers published in 2004,[1] one of the questions the interviewers asked was, "Should there be a Third Vatican Council?" Almost everyone said no.[2]

They said no almost entirely for the same reasons, too. The opinion of those who were present at the Second Vatican Council was that the church still has a lot of work to do in order to realize the teachings of Vatican II. The vision remains compelling. Despite all obstacles along the way, the path ahead lies open. We are far from finished. Those who knew its vision best, because they saw it develop first-hand, believed this to be true. There is, in fact, nothing more important than to continue the work of Vatican II.

With respect to the Constitution on the Sacred Liturgy, what is the state of the questions? It is clear that the Constitution on the Sacred Liturgy has had a profound and lasting effect on the church in our time. It continues to give shape to Catholic understanding and practice, and to inspire as well as direct the actions of the faithful with respect to the liturgy. Over the years some of its provisions, such as the restoration of the prayer of the faithful or the increased use of sacred scripture in the liturgy, have simply come to be taken for granted. Other items, such as communion from the cup or the use of Gregorian chant, have had their ups and downs as the church struggles to give robust expression to its liturgical rites in the present day. A number of the document's key assertions, for example those concerning the paschal mystery or active participation, have been well accepted and continue to generate lively interest. Still others, such as the principle of inculturation and the use of vernacular languages in the liturgy, continue to pose new challenges. Is it possible to summarize where the church is at present, in the midst of such a vast array of issues and questions?

There are a number of different ways to review the state of the questions implicit in the document *Sacrosanctum Concilium*. We will attempt two approaches. First, we will turn to the seven essential concepts described in Part II, evaluate the degree of their acceptance, and identify areas of potential growth they contain. Second, we will return to where the document itself begins, namely, the broad aims of the council. The reform of the liturgy was cast as an integral expression of the council's mission and purpose. It seems appropriate therefore to ask how well it has done its work to date with respect to the four goals of the council stated in its preamble. As this is the broadest base from which to evaluate the state of the questions, it will serve as a concluding summary.

SEVEN ESSENTIAL CONCEPTS

1. The Paschal Mystery

The seven key concepts of the Constitution on the Sacred Liturgy stand at different levels of acceptance. The first of these, the centrality of the paschal mystery, has enjoyed the greatest acceptance. Alone among all the voices that have commented on the reform of the liturgy since the council, the Society of Saint Pius X (Lefèbvrites) maintains that the council's use of the theology of the paschal mystery has undermined the true meaning of the Mass.[3] Other than this schismatic group, however, no one has mounted a serious challenge to this concept. Indeed, it has been fully embraced.

Evidence of its acceptance can be seen at all levels. All of the church's ritual books and catechetical documents make reference to it. The official pronouncements of popes and bishops appeal to it often as a matter of fundamental importance and a basis for wide agreement. It is also fair to say that the Catholic imagination has been caught by it. Catholics will tell you that the Mass is about Christ *crucified and risen*. It would not occur to them to object, as some of the council fathers did, that the Mass is concerned only with the sacrifice of the cross. The memorial acclamation, in the heart of the Eucharistic Prayer, claims this ground definitively. Outside of the liturgy too, the idea of the paschal mystery has exerted an influence in popular religious writings, in works of spirituality, and in art and music. It may even be responsible for a certain affective tone that can be observed in the church since the Second Vatican Council, a joy that arises from grasping the death and resurrection of Christ as two inseparable aspects of the one mystery we celebrate.

A perennial challenge that remains is for the faithful to continue to develop an inner adherence to that mystery. As we saw earlier, Burkhard Neunheuser, OSB, observed that a hallmark of the liturgy should be that it enables the people to *live* the paschal mystery. It is one thing to reverently recall the life, death, and resurrection of Jesus; it is another to give ourselves over to living this mystery. Catholics readily affirm that "Christ has died, Christ is risen, Christ will come again." Yet there is still, for many, a journey to be traveled so as to be able to say with conviction: "Dying you destroyed *our* death" and "rising you restored *our* life…" [emphasis added]. This is the ongoing pastoral challenge of appropriating what the liturgy celebrates.

It is most likely that the church will reach deeper levels of appropriation of the paschal mystery only through the broad application of an experiential catechesis which takes mystery seriously. Instruction in dogma can only go so far in this realm. To appropriate a mystery, one needs mystagogical catechesis.

Fortunately, the church has some splendid historical precedents as well as current applications in the area of mystagogical catechesis that it may draw upon to help meet this challenge. On no fewer than three separate occasions, Pope John Paul II called for a recovery of "the art of mystagogic catechesis" upon the liturgy.[4] By this "art" he most certainly had in mind that form of catechesis which flourished in the patristic era. In the ancient church, mystagogical catechesis drew people, through the signs and symbols of the liturgical rites, into the heart of the mystery the liturgy celebrates—the paschal mystery. As Father David Regan, CSSp, of Brazil, observed in his book, *Experience the Mystery: Pastoral Possibilities for Christian Mystagogy*, there has been a resurgence of interest in mystagogy since the council. He delineates three types: liturgical mystagogy, mystagogy for men and women in whom the modern secular world has provoked a crisis of religion, and the mystagogy of mysticism.[5] The Lineamenta for the 2005 Synod of Bishops signaled the importance of this subject by including a chapter on "The Eucharistic Mystagogy for the New Evangelization."[6] Clearly, interest is growing in this area, still new to the church in our time; it will be a development to watch.

Looking ahead, another development that could take place is a shift in how the church celebrates the three sacraments of initiation: baptism, confirmation, and Eucharist. The council fathers were concerned to reassert the fundamental unity of these three sacraments. The unity of the initiation sacraments was seen as an important theological principle to be recovered and cherished by the whole church. (The unity of initiation has been maintained by the Eastern rite churches. In the West however, due to accidents of history, the celebration of these three sacraments has been divided into separate occasions since the Middle Ages.) Consequently, all the reformed rites of initiation that were produced after the council—the *Rite of Christian Initiation of Adults*, the *Rite of Baptism for Children*, and the *Rite of Confirmation*—make attempts to recover a sense of this unity.

In the reformed initiation rites for adults and children of catechetical age, the unity of the three sacraments was very obviously affirmed by restoring the practice of celebrating all three together in a single ceremony. Also, in the Latin rite, on those occasions when the sacraments are celebrated at intervals separated by some years (as in the case of infant baptism, with later confirmation and Eucharist), the new ritual texts emerging from the council have appealed for at least some acknowledgment of the unity of these three sacraments in the ritual itself. At infant baptism, for example, the eventual confirmation and communion of the infant is explicitly named by words that are spoken when the infant is brought to the altar. In the celebration of confirmation, baptismal promises are renewed, and frequently the Eucharist is celebrated too. These were attempts to regain a broader appreciation of the unity of these sacraments.

Paragraph 215 of the *Rite of Christian Initiation of Adults* goes so far as to say that the link between baptism and confirmation is rooted in the paschal mystery itself: "the conjunction of the two celebrations signifies the unity of the paschal mystery, the close link between the mission of the Son and the outpouring of the Holy Spirit, and the connection between the two sacraments through which the Son and the Holy Spirit come with the Father to those who are baptized."

This assertion invites greater reflection. If it were taken more to heart, the initial attempts at bringing the sacraments of initiation into closer relation could gain new momentum. At the very least, there would be more grappling with the theological questions that lie at the foundations of our sacramental practice. Right now, the church is in a "both/and" situation, where two different models of how to bring people into the full sacramental life of the church exist side by side. The Latin rite Catholic Church now commonly celebrates the three sacraments on separate occasions—spanning the period from infancy through childhood—for children of Catholic parents. At the same time, it celebrates the three sacraments together in one event for those whose initiation is prescribed by the Rite of Christian Initiation of Adults.

An overall change of practice—that is to say, the idea of reuniting in a single celebration the sacraments of initiation for *all* Catholics— would have been unthinkable at the time of the council. Even now, such an idea would be considered a radical proposal. The fundamental question of how well our present arrangement of the initiation sacraments accords with our theology, however, is one that may be posed anew precisely in light of the strong acceptance of the notion of the paschal mystery. As it is expressed in *Rite of Christian Initiation of Adults*, paragraph 215, the concept of the paschal mystery provides a powerful incentive for re-examining our initiatory practice. Nothing will happen quickly in this realm, but it is another place to watch for long-term developments.

2. Liturgy as "Summit and Source" of the Church's Life

It would be hard to find another center of the church's life to compete with the liturgy as "summit and source," and yet it seems that acceptance of this concept since Vatican II has been more shallow than acceptance of the paschal mystery. Certainly, the idea enjoys formal acceptance, and there are devout Catholics everywhere who would agree that it speaks for their experience. But there are other indications that suggest it has not made as much of a difference as might have been expected.

For example, the number of Catholics worldwide who do not attend Sunday Mass regularly is significant.[7] Leaving aside those who have no access to Mass because of the priest shortage and those who have consciously renounced their faith, there are still many who think of themselves as Catholics but who simply opt out of the community's worship on a regular basis. They may come to church for marriage and funerals and to secure the first sacraments of their children, but they are content otherwise to stay away. Either the liturgy is not, for them, the summit and source of Christian life, or they have an attenuated sense of what this means.

The liturgy today "competes" with all sorts of lesser activities that vie for the attention of Catholics on Sunday. For liturgy to take precedence over all other options, attendance must certainly be cultivated in a way never before dreamed necessary. In many instances, the work of persuading our own people of the centrality of the liturgy simply hasn't been done.[8] Will the next generation really be drawn to affirm the liturgy as summit and source by the witness they see today? This is a big question.

Another factor that compromises the ability of the liturgy to serve as the true summit and source of Christian life today is the existence of disunity and polarization within the church. When individuals or groups feel themselves alienated by particular teachings or church policies, or by the church's involvement in civil politics, disaffection from the liturgy often follows. Liturgy becomes, perhaps, a thing to be argued over, but not the summit nor the source of a common life. Such situations are complex and often fraught with very real and valid concerns. Nevertheless, the effect of presenting or viewing the liturgy as the property of a particular party or the tool of an agenda can be devastating.

How serious is the church about fostering unity and reconciliation, so that people can worship together in peace? This is another big question.

One unfortunate sign that liturgy is not treated as summit and source of the church's life is the lack of continuing institutional support for liturgical renewal. After initial efforts at reform and a flourishing of interest after the council, it seems that fewer resources have been given to the unfinished work of liturgical renewal overall. The United States, for example, has witnessed in recent years a pattern of bishops closing diocesan worship offices and reducing the activities of liturgical commissions. In terms of budget priorities, liturgy has certainly not been the last item to be sacrificed, but indeed one of the first!

It could be argued that this is not a symptom of any lack of regard for the liturgy, but rather a sign that the machinery of the liturgy is well-oiled and functioning at the parish level without the aid of diocesan personnel. This argument is implausible. Activities regarded as important in any community are supported institutionally. It would be considered foolish, for example, to expect a Catholic school system to flourish without superintendents. No one in diocesan administration sincerely believes that fund-raising or building maintenance should be left to chance. Yet liturgy is expected to bear the weight of being the "summit and source" of Christian life quasi-automatically. Everything depends upon the action of Christ in the liturgy, it is true. But we are still obligated to support it institutionally.

Finally, on the parish level, the amount of time given by pastors to the preparation of liturgy and preaching simply does not uniformly reflect the kind of priority one would expect it to have, if the constitution's vision were truly believed and embraced. There are notable exceptions, and the priority given to liturgy as the "summit and source" of the church's life in some places is indeed very high. In general, however, this is an area where work remains to be done. Reflection on the constitution itself can help the church today to keep its priorities clear.

3. Full, Active, and Conscious Participation

Of all the concepts found in the constitution, the one that enjoyed the greatest momentum going into the council was "full, active, conscious participation." The idea had been gathering steam since 1903 when

Pope Pius X first wrote about it. Vigorously promoted by Lambert Beauduin, OSB, and many others in the liturgical movement, it was the impetus behind many practical initiatives (such as the publication of missals with vernacular translations that the people could follow, dialogue Masses, experiments with the priest facing the people, and so on) even before the council began. Afterwards, it was energetically applied in the making of the reform, as parts for the people were written into every one of the church's rites and participation was encouraged at every level.

The principle enjoys a very high degree of acceptance as the ideal toward which the church continues to strive. This does not mean the goal has been reached. Obviously, not everyone actively participates in the liturgy today in those ways that are observable (such as spoken and sung prayer). It is easy to imagine too that a fair number fail to accomplish that inward participation which was also the council's goal. But no one today would say, as Pope Pius XII found it easy to do, that some people are incapable of participating in the liturgy and should just engage in other pious exercises while Mass is going on (*MD*, 108).

From the loftiest church pronouncements to the humblest parish liturgy committee discussions, it is widely agreed that the participation of all is expected. The liturgical reforms that followed the council created a liturgy that was not too arcane or difficult for ordinary people to understand or appreciate. The role of the assembly is not beyond the capacities of the average Catholic. The goal is therefore also seen as achievable; it is not an impossible dream. Thus, when parish musicians work on strategies to increase congregational singing, when religious educators work with parents to help them take part in their children's first sacraments with understanding and faith, when hospitality ministers ask how they can help create a welcoming environment for worship, they are each in their own way entering the same discussion: How do we achieve that full, active, conscious participation called for by the council? One may disagree with the strategies any given individual or group comes up with, but all are agreed that they want to achieve what the constitution asked.

In an area where a lot of efforts are being made, naturally some mistakes are made too. Problems in this area tend to fall into two types: the tendency toward effusion or the tendency toward minimalism. An example of the effusive tendency would be the practice that arose spontaneously in some places in the 1970s of having the assembly say parts of the Eucharistic Prayer along with the priest. The question of full participation in the Eucharistic Prayer is, of course, poorly addressed by having everyone speak the words together in chorus, and this practice has been suppressed.

At the other end of the spectrum is the tendency to invoke the principle of inward, *spiritual* participation as a kind of excuse for minimal outward participation from the congregation. When the people don't utter the responses or the choir director wants the choir alone to sing settings of the people's parts of the Mass, well, who is to say the assembly is not participating spiritually? Yet the role of the assembly is easily compromised by such excuses or inappropriate decisions. The constitution enjoined more than once that the people's "hearts be attuned to their voices," not that their voices should be silent or that the choir or other ministers be used as a surrogate.

Spiritual participation in the liturgy is, of course, very important. In his book, *The Spirit of the Liturgy*, Cardinal Joseph Ratzinger (now Pope Benedict XVI) countered the shallow view that participation may be measured solely by external activity by drawing attention to the *actio* of Christ's sacrifice as what the believer is called to share in the liturgy.[9] Participation, he argues, is not so much a matter of having more people in the gifts procession as it is of being taken up spiritually in the action of Christ at the altar.

Pope John Paul II entered the discussion in a somewhat different way, calling attention to the importance of silence in the liturgy, not as the absence of participation, but as a profound aspect of it. Pope John Paul II, in his apostolic letter *Dies Domini*, also drew out the theological dynamics of participation by describing what takes place between God and his people in the Liturgy of the Word as a dialogue (*DD*, 40–41).[10] The pope made it explicit that participation in the Liturgy of the Word is intended to lead to a personal response of faith and renewed commitment to continuing conversion—spiritual outcomes that make a visible difference in the world outside of liturgy but which begin during the liturgy in an inward and invisible way.

Future development of the concept of full, active, and conscious participation will no doubt be influenced by advances in the study of human culture. Although it is clear that our sense of participation is culturally conditioned, it is less clear what the implications of such conditioning may be for the celebration of liturgy in specific local settings. It seems that conversation about what participation is, how it is fostered, and what criteria we use to discern it will continue to be lively.

4. Ecclesiology

The greatest progress made under this heading has been in retrieving a sense of the dignity of baptism. The restoration of the rites of the catechumenate, the return of adult baptism to the heart of the liturgical year in the Easter Vigil, along with the renewal of the rite of baptism for infants, have had a definite impact on the church's sense of itself as a whole. The rites of initiation of adults especially, by integrating all aspects of initiation into a unified vision of church life, have done much to renew Catholic ecclesiology. It remains a challenge to broaden the base of communities that make full use of the reformed initiation rites. In many parts of the world the adult catechumenate is still rarely seen or used incompletely. Nevertheless, the move has been made in principle, and where it is also achieved in practice the results have been most encouraging.

The active participation of the laity in the liturgy at every level, including liturgical ministries that are now considered proper to them, has also been well accepted—indeed, the implementation of such lay involvement in the liturgy has been more widespread than implementation of the full reform of baptism. Although lingering manifestations of clericalism are still present in the church today, there is a general acknowledgment of the idea that liturgies are not private functions, that the assembly is part of the action, and that the liturgical event is always, even in small assemblies, an image of the church. The fruit of having cultivated "full, active, conscious participation" is being harvested in celebrations all over the world. In sum, as a result of the reforms of Vatican II, the church is much further along in developing a sense of the dignity of baptism and the integral role of the laity in the liturgy.

The renewed vision of the ministry of the bishop has been less successful. Attempts have been made, but problems remain. The role of bishops' conferences, much encouraged by the document, is also currently at a low ebb. Two main reasons for the limited success of the renewed role of the bishop suggest themselves. First, the size of dioceses is so large that it is virtually impossible for a bishop to maintain a pastoral presence that is liturgically based and centered on the Eucharist, as the constitution so beautifully presented it. Contact with the bishop for most people tends to be either nonliturgical—through letters, fund-raising appeals, television, and the like—or else it is extremely rare, such as at the Rite of Election (which is frequently held at a word service) or the celebration of the sacrament of confirmation in parishes. Many bishops would like to be more present to their people as the quintessential presider at the Eucharist in their diocese, with all the orders of the church gathered around them, but the odds are simply against it. The liturgy remains an icon of a community of faith and prayer, but is not in any real sense an icon of the local church gathered around its bishop.

Second, in recent years Rome has tried to centralize liturgical decision-making, and the bishop's role has been diminished as a result. Two examples illustrate this trend. First, not only did Rome demand the re-constitution of ICEL so as to closely supervise liturgical translations that had previously been supervised by bishops, but *Liturgiam Authenticam* goes so far as to say that Rome reserves the right to produce translations *on its own* if it does not find acceptable the ones approved by the bishops. The bishops are then obliged to promulgate these translations in their territory (*LA*, 104; compare with *SC*, 22.2 and 36.4). There is not much collegiality evident in a regulation of this kind. Second, *Redemptionis Sacramentum* enjoins the faithful to report liturgical abuses not only to their bishop but also directly to the Holy See (*RS*, 184). It afterwards adds that the diocesan bishop should be informed first "insofar as it is possible" (why it might not be possible is unclear) as a matter of *charity*. But there seems to be little concern for undermining the bishop's *authority* in liturgical matters by establishing this pipeline to the Vatican. To be sure, the tendency to centralize is nothing new, but it has new tools at its disposal and therefore new temptations. With the development of modern technologies of communication, there arises a great temptation for Rome to bypass local authorities by appealing directly to the Catholic population, as well as a temptation for individuals to bypass local authorities by appealing directly to Rome.

Thus, both of these recent documents have expressed a trend toward the diminution of the role of the local bishop and of groups of bishops in liturgical regulation, which the council document had sought to expand. This necessarily affects the ecclesiological balance. The vision of church that the constitution put forth could again be strengthened, but it remains to be seen whether there is the will to do this in the church today.

5. Inculturation

The Constitution on the Sacred Liturgy used the word "adaptation" to describe what happens to the liturgy when it becomes a living part of the various human cultures. Since the council, a shift to the term "inculturation" has taken place. This has now become the standard way of naming the concerns of articles 37–40. The 1994 instruction on the right implementation of the Constitution on the Sacred Liturgy, *Inculturation and the Roman Liturgy*, gives cause for hope that the way promised by *Sacrosanctum Concilium* remains open.

Thanks to the provisions of the constitution concerning the inculturation of the liturgy, a number of Catholic communities around the globe have made progress in developing their own ways of celebrating the liturgy. Indeed, by proposing acceptance of liturgical diversity on a broad scale, these paragraphs have had an effect on the whole Catholic world. When the African Synod, which took place in Rome in 1994, used the Zairian rite at St. Peter's Basilica, it gave powerful witness to the worldwide church of what liturgical inculturation can mean. After all, it is not every day that one sees cardinals dancing in St. Peter's![11]

At present, however, there appear to be considerable reservations in Rome about liturgical inculturation. Neither the post-synodal decree *Ecclesia in Africa* (1995) nor *Ecclesia in Asia* (1999) gave more than a single paragraph to inculturation of the liturgy. Despite extensive discussion of cultures in *Ecclesia in Oceania* (2001), liturgical inculturation received but one muted and apologetic reference (in no. 39). In *Ecclesia in America* (1999) and *Ecclesia in Europa* (2003), it was not even mentioned.

It would be a mistake, however, to deduce from these documents that the bishops of the world, or their flocks, are uninterested in further developments toward inculturation of the liturgy. It is natural for inculturation to proceed "from below," with initiatives arising in specific local contexts and only gradually gaining official recognition. In the words of John Mansford Prior, SVD, a missionary for many years in Indonesia and consultor to the Pontifical Council for Culture,

We are now becoming increasingly aware that inculturation of worship and spirituality does not begin with church commissions, with experts and officials who decide what elements of local culture should be adapted to a framework imported from the West.... Authentic liturgy and spirituality celebrate what is most beautiful, most real, and most important in life. We celebrate what we believe, our innermost convictions, that for which we are ready to live and die.[12]

As an example of this, he described a Good Friday service held in Maumere on Flores Island that has become legendary in that place. It followed a series of devastating events: first, an earthquake and tidal wave hit the island, leaving twenty-six hundred people dead and most public buildings destroyed. Later, tensions erupted between the townspeople of Maumere and the army. Finally, troops surrounded a section of the town, beat everyone up, and an innocent young Muslim man, a visitor to the town, was killed.

The Good Friday service following these traumatic events, precisely because of the way in which it was inculturated, moved the people of that town from anger and the desire for revenge to solidarity and peace. The gospel was proclaimed at a series of stations: "Over five thousand people gathered outside the mayor's office to hear of Pilate washing his hands. We moved to the police station to hear of Peter's denial. Then we moved to the military barracks to hear of Jesus' condemnation. The procession came to a climax as we meditated upon the death of Jesus at the place where the Muslim was beaten to death."[13] Sin was named, and sinners were called to repentance. The liturgical signs and symbols of Good Friday took on profound new dimensions and became part of that community's story and life.

After Good Friday 1993 the cross has come to mean willingness to suffer with the persecuted, of taking the consequences of speaking the truth in a world of deceit. Since Good Friday 1993 people have been retelling the event, spontaneously in their local languages, in their own images and proverbs, saying in their own tongues what Paul discovered in his life, "when I am weak, then I am strong" (2 Cor. 12:10).[14]

Such an event flies beneath the radar scope of papal and curial statements, but is nonetheless a real response to the council's call to inculturate the liturgy.

Reflection upon inculturation of the liturgy has been accumulating and maturing since the council. The scholarly work of Anscar Chupungco, OSB, of the Philippines, who taught for many years at the Pontifical Liturgical Institute in Rome, is particularly noteworthy.[15] The topic has broadened in various ways too. As Aylward Shorter, MAfr, has observed, the transformation of a culture by the complete integration of Christian faith should result not only in creating indigenous expressions of the Roman rite, but also in Christianizing traditional rites already present and cherished within the culture.[16]

There has been a growing realization since the council that inculturation of the liturgy must reflect the whole reality of the Christianization of a culture. Christianization is not a form of imperialism, but a transformation through which a civilization realizes its own deepest identity by means of faith. An eclectic approach to liturgical inculturation therefore—taking bits of one culture and inserting them into a liturgy that remains the expression of a different culture—fails to recognize the true dimensions of the challenge of inculturation. Indeed, the constitution's provision for the inculturation of the liturgy contains perhaps the greatest unrealized potential of all the essential concepts of the document we have discussed. New dimensions of the task are still being discovered.

A resounding affirmation of the inculturation that has already taken place was voiced at the Extraordinary Synod on the Eucharist in Rome in 2005 by the president of the symposium of the episcopal conferences of Africa and Madagascar, John Olorunfemi Onaiyekan, archbishop of Abuja, Nigeria. His statement contains hope for the future:

> My intervention is a hymn of praise and thanksgiving to God for the great blessings that the Church in Africa has enjoyed in the Post Vatican II era through the "active, conscious, fruitful" and indeed also joyous participation in the Eucharist celebrated in the richness of our cultural expressions.... All over Africa, in the last forty years, beautiful eucharistic celebrations have emerged which have deepened the faith of the people,

improved the quality of their participation, increased the love for the priesthood, given joy and hope in the midst of distress and despair, fostered ecumenical rapport, and generally promoted evangelization. The Eucharist deserves—and is receiving—the best of our cultures. We may not have much to offer in terms of the glorious architecture of European cathedrals or the fabulous paintings of Michelangelo and Leonardo da Vinci. But what we have, we are happy to give: our songs and lyrics, our drumming and rhythmic body movements, all to the glory of God. We do well to acknowledge and extol the valuable heritage of the eucharistic traditions of the different ancient rites of both the East and the West. I believe these are themselves products of an inculturation that took place many centuries ago under the guidance of the Holy Spirit. That same Spirit has not gone to sleep.[17]

Because of the growth of the church in Africa and Asia since the council,[18] the significance of inculturation has become even greater.

6. Renewal of the Liturgical Books, Music, Art, and Artifacts of the Liturgy

An enormous amount of work has gone into fulfilling the council's mandate for the renewal of the books, music, art, and artifacts of the liturgy. Nearly everything done in this area has been contested, yet genuine change has happened and been accepted. We reviewed these developments in a general way in the last chapter. Careful studies of the elements involved in realizing this imperative of the council are available for those who wish to learn more.[19]

The pace of liturgical change immediately after the council was extremely rapid. In the years following, it has slowed. This slowdown is natural and to the benefit of everyone, as change without rest can be disorienting and enervating for a community. Nevertheless, a process of more gradual development has not stopped. One of the great virtues of the reform was that it took a dynamic view of the liturgy. An ongoing process of refinement of rites, music, art, and so on, requiring both critical and creative work, is supported by the constitution. That work continues. Although our era is not likely to see another great influx of major changes, it is normal to see a steady process of minor revision of the liturgy as it is needed.

Of the reforms that have taken place, several particular items stand out as areas that have not yet reached their peak. As Father Pierre-Marie Gy, OP, a peritus at the council, observed, "Two other things that are developing but are not yet fully realized are the assimilation of the eucharistic prayer...and Communion under two kinds."[20] Gy was concerned about cultivating a deeper appreciation for the Eucharistic Prayer in pastors who are celebrating the liturgy. The same might also be said for the faithful. The Eucharistic Prayer is rarely treated in religious education textbooks or as the subject of preaching. Adult Catholics commonly have never been taught much about it, or invited to reflect on and marvel at how rich an expression it is.

Is a greater appreciation of the Eucharistic Prayer really an urgent need in the church today? Some would say yes. A positive reason for this is that it is the great prayer of the Mass; we need the full benefit of its theological richness to dawn upon us and draw us deeply into union with the Trinity in the act of praying it. All are expected to join their individual prayers with it, uniting their offering of their own lives with the offering of the sacrifice on the altar. These are the positive reasons for seeking a deeper awareness of this prayer.

On the negative side, a failure to assimilate the Eucharistic Prayer leads to distortions. For example, when communion services became a more frequent occurrence in the United States as a result of the priest shortage, liturgists and bishops alike were dismayed to discover that many of the faithful couldn't tell the difference between a communion service and Mass. The absence of the Eucharistic Prayer did not make much of an impression, as long as people got communion! There was a hue and cry about suppressing communion services, largely because laypeople (including women) were leading them, but at the same time an opportunity was missed. No sustained attention was given to the need for developing among Catholics a greater sense of the whole Eucharistic Prayer. Here is a treasure waiting to be discovered.

The same could be said for communion from the chalice. A tremendous richness has become available to Catholics through the reintroduction of communion under both forms, yet that richness and the spiritual benefits offered through this practice are not always reflected upon or valued as highly as they should be. The practice often languishes as a mere option, and pastoral discussions concerning it dwell more on microbiology and disease control than they do on theology and spirituality.

The inspiring intervention of Father Barry Fischer, CPPS, general moderator of the Missionaries of the Most Precious Blood, at the 2005 Synod of Bishops, shows that there are exceptions to this generalization, however:

> The communion achieved in the reconciling Blood of Christ empowers us to be bridgebuilders, truth-tellers, and the healers of wounds. Our "amen" when receiving communion affirms not only the real presence of Christ in the Eucharist; it invites us to be bread broken and blood poured out, life given, for the life of the world. We become as it were "living chalices" carrying the Precious Blood of Christ, that sacred balm, to those who are in need of healing in their brokenness, to those wounded by poverty, to those left half dead by the wayside, scorned and scarred by prejudice, racism, and war.[21]

A determination to continue support for communion from the chalice was also much in evidence in the words of Bishop Robert Lynch, of the Diocese of St. Petersburg Florida, when he addressed leaders from Diocesan Liturgical Commissions across the United States in a meeting hosted by the Federation of Diocesan Liturgical Commissions and the American bishops in October of 2004. He said, of preserving this practice: "That would be the 'liturgical ditch' that I might choose to die in were that also some time in the future to be forbidden or limited."[22]

Finally, the continuing progress of the implementation of the *Rite of Christian Initiation of Adults* will be something to watch. If the first waves of this development are any indication, it will have a renewing effect on the church as a whole as it proceeds to broader implementation. Although a tendency among bishops to regard the process of initiation as primarily an educational endeavor has detracted from its true genius, it continues to hold immense promise for the church as a liturgical reform involving the entire community of faith. Its rites are impressive, and in the act of carrying them out the church comes to a new awareness of itself and its mission.

7. Education and Formation

A complete and up-to-date picture of the state of liturgical education and formation of clergy around the world is, unfortunately, not available. Even on a local level, in the United States, questions regarding the implementation of *Sacrosanctum Concilium's* articles 15–18 have not been thoroughly explored. The data we have shows a mixed picture. A survey of U.S. seminaries taken in 1995 by the Federation of Diocesan Liturgical Commissions, for example, showed that seven out of forty-one seminaries (17 percent) offered no liturgical formation, or non-credit offerings, or only one course given in a single year. On the other hand, twenty of the responses (49 percent) represented the high end of the spectrum, with courses offered either for every year or for three out of four years of studies. The rest were in the middle. Thus, the situation in the United States seems to have improved considerably in a number of seminaries between 1975 and 1995, but it nevertheless continues to fall short overall of the mandate of the constitution that "[t]he study of sacred liturgy is to be ranked among the compulsory and major courses in seminaries and religious houses of studies; in theological faculties it is to rank among the principal courses" (*SC*, 16).[23]

A firm answer to the question of whether or not seminary professors in other fields relate their disciplines to the liturgy as a means of unifying all priestly training, as article 16 demands, remains elusive as well. Anecdotal evidence again suggests a mixed picture. The same can be said for the continuing education of clergy (*SC*, 18) and liturgical formation of the laity (*SC*, 19). Laudable efforts are being made, yet certainly more could be done.

Since the time of the council, the landscape of ministry has changed somewhat, with a decline in numbers of religious, a rise in lay ministry, and the growth of the permanent deaconate. In recent years especially, there has been tremendous growth in the number of permanent deacons and lay ecclesial ministers serving the church worldwide. The 2000 *Annuarium Statisticum Ecclesiae* showed a fourfold increase in the number of permanent deacons between 1978 and 2000, and a *forty-four-fold* increase in the number of "lay missionaries" between 1990 and 2000 alone.[24] The number of catechists, another lay category, grew by 48 percent during that same ten-year period. So, while seminary education and priestly formation in the liturgy continue to be crucial, the presence of so many "workers in the vineyard" who are neither priests nor vowed religious suggests that a commitment to their formation and education in liturgy is also important for the future of the liturgical reform. In order to fulfill the spirit of the council's mandate, and not only its letter, this issue will need to be addressed.

THE OVERALL GOALS OF THE COUNCIL: CONCLUDING SUMMARY

The goals of the council as stated in the introduction to the Constitution on the Sacred Liturgy can be summed up as follows: the council was to renew God's people, update the church to the times, foster unity among all Christians, and promote the spread of the gospel to the whole world. The reform and renewal of the liturgy was, and remains, integral to this vast and noble project.

In the process of becoming more attuned to the times and more engaged with the work of ecumenism and evangelization, the church, living organism that it is, has had to grow and change, drawing deeply from the source of its life. The reformed liturgy of Vatican II has facilitated this growth; it has been a fruitful reform. As a result of the reform, the church has certainly been enriched, modernized, and made more capable of ecumenical and evangelizing efforts across the board. It has grown by fits and starts, it has made missteps along the way, but it has not failed, and it has not turned back.

In the intervening period since the council, the church has at times encountered great resistance in keeping the outward-directed vision that the preamble voiced. The liturgical reform's ecumenical advances have been decried as "Protestantizing tendencies," its impulse toward evangelization as "insufficiently doctrinal," its updating to the times as "modernist heresy," and its renewal of God's people as spurious. Yet the renewal has persisted, with the liturgy at its heart. The numbers of priests and religious may be down, but the number of Catholics overall is up, and their fervor is palpable. The ranks of those serving the church have swelled with growth in the numbers of permanent deacons and lay ecclesial ministers. Where evangelization is practiced and the *Rite of Christian Initiation of Adults* is implemented, the number of converts is also rising. Prescinding from the many details of the liturgical reform and looking at the whole: Are we better off liturgically now than we were forty years ago? Of course we are. It would be a great irony indeed if, after all that has been accomplished, we should lose confidence now in the principles that inspired the reforms of Vatican II or in the reforms themselves.

Of all the aspects of the council's agenda, the one that seems today to be most cast into doubt by the prevailing mood or climate in the church is the idea of updating to the times. In her official pronouncements, and unofficial grumblings, the church today seems ever more inclined to blame our ills on the evil days in which we live rather than to seek out the good that is within them. In the realm of liturgy, this impulse expresses itself as a "rush to platonism"[25]—a desire for a timeless liturgy, for a liturgy that gives us access to a divine world untouched by the grime of history. Why update to the times, if the world as we know it is passing away? In recent years committees have gotten busy revising the translations of liturgical texts to assure they will use a "sacral" language to express "eternal realities." Even words like "cup" are suppressed as "profane." Workshops are held about "the heavenly liturgy," as if someone had access to the order of worship there. We search for tokens of eschatology in the liturgy as though looking for clues of a suppressed inheritance in *The DaVinci Code*.

I appreciate the importance of eschatology in the liturgy, but I worry about what we miss if we do not continue to concern ourselves, even now, with "updating to the times." Neither Pope John XXIII nor the council fathers demanded that the church update itself either because they thought the times were rosy or because they expected this world to last forever. Rather, the call to *aggiornamento* arose from the moral imperative to proclaim the gospel in the world we really inhabit and to love the people whom we actually have as neighbors. These continue to be imperatives for the church, as the world around us—and we ourselves—continue to change. The times in which we live cannot fail to have a profound effect on how we worship. It is best to acknowledge them.

The liturgy should indeed get us ready for heaven, but not for the heaven of the neoplatonists. The heaven for which liturgy prepares us is the one we can reach only by immersion in the paschal mystery, which is incarnate in the grimy reality of sin and grace in human history. By such an immersion we find, and in the end become, the Body of Christ, radiant and risen, with all our wounds made glorious.

NOTES

PART I: THE DOCUMENTS

1. "...[T]he whole conception was in the style of Leo XIII....Perhaps the idea was to make clear the *terminus a quo* in matters liturgical!" Josef Jungmann, quoted by Andrea Riccardi in "The Tumultuous Opening Days of the Council," *History of Vatican II, Volume II: The Formation of the Council's Identity, First Period and Intercession, October 1962–September 1963*, ed. Giuseppe Alberigo and Joseph Komonchak (Maryknoll, NY: Orbis, and Leuven: Peeters, 1997), 12.

2. "Sacra Tridentina Synodus," 20 December 1905.

3. Bernard Botte, *From Silence to Participation: An Insider's View of Liturgical Renewal* (Washington, DC: The Pastoral Press, 1988), 3.

4. Botte, 86.

5. Louis Bouyer, *Liturgical Piety* (Notre Dame: University of Notre Dame Press, 1955), 1–9.

6. Romano Guardini, "A Letter from Romano Guardini," *Herder Correspondence 1: Special Issue* (1964) 24.

7. The Sacerdotal Communities of Saint-Severin of Paris and Saint-Joseph of Nice, *The Liturgical Movement* (New York: Hawthorne Books, 1964), 13.

8. *Mediator Dei*, 61–64.

9. *Tra le Sollecitudini*, 220.

10. Keith Pecklers, *The Unread Vision: The Liturgical Movement in the United States of America: 1926–1955* (Collegeville, MN: Liturgical Press, 1998), 81 ff.

11. These included the revision of the psalter, the practice of frequent communion and lowering of the age of first communion, new norms for church music, and changes to the missal that were implemented in 1920 by Pope Benedict XV.

12. *Mediator Dei*, 80.

13. *Mediator Dei*, 86.

14. *Mediator Dei*, 118.

15. *Mediator Dei*, 43.

16. Annibale Bugnini, *The Reform of the Liturgy: 1948–1975* (Collegeville, MN: Liturgical Press, 1990), note 1, 7. There is some evidence that Pope Pius XII was thinking about a general reform as early as 1942.

17. Detailed footnotes providing background for the changes in this and the other liturgies of Holy Week were published by two members of the Pian commission, Annibale Bugnini and Carlo Braga, in 1956. In 1957, Herman Schmidt published an extensive study of the same liturgies in two volumes. Unfortunately for the non-specialist, these informative works are entirely in Latin. They are also out of print.

18. Yet even this was not entirely without historical precedent. The *pascha annotinum* or anniversary remembrance of baptism is attested by some ancient writers. A. Bugnini and C. Braga, *Ordo Hebdomadae Sanctae Instauratus* (Rome: Edizioni Liturgiche, 1956), 137 ff.

19. Frederick MacManus, *The Rites of Holy Week* (Patterson, NJ: St. Anthony Guild Press, 1956, 1957), vi–vii.

20. Bugnini, 10.

21. *The Assisi Papers: Proceedings of the First International Congress of Pastoral Liturgy, Assisi-Rome, September 18–22, 1956* (Collegeville, MN: Liturgical Press, 1957), 224.

22. Bugnini, 14–15. Description of the work leading up to the final form of the document is based on Bugnini's account, unless otherwise noted.

23. Monsignor Anglés also exhibited paranoia about Communists, and for this reason refused to send materials to a Polish bishop assigned to his committee.

24. Botte, who was a consultor to this committee, reported that, to his knowledge, it never met. He therefore submitted in writing some of his own thoughts, which were reworked into a report by the head of the committee, Monsignor Borella of Milan. The report was submitted but never used. Botte, 120–21. Borella's report may be "the rather muddled text" to which Bugnini refers on page 24.

25. Mathijs Lamberigts, "The Liturgy Debate," *History of Vatican II, Volume II*, 120.

26. Spellman had also resisted carrying out the reform of the Easter Vigil in 1951 but was forced into implementing it by Pope Pius XII. Pierre-Marie Gy, OP, interview by Michael Driscoll in *Voices from the Council*, ed. Michael R. Prendergast and M. D. Ridge (Portland, OR: Pastoral Press, 2004), 152.

27. Lamberigts, 126. Ottaviani advocated dropping paragraph 37 altogether.

28. Bugnini, 24.

29. Botte, 119–21.

30. Pope Paul VI, address *Tempus Iam Advenit* at the end of the second session of Vatican II (December 4, 1964), in *The Pope Speaks* 9 (1963–64), 224.

PART II: MAJOR POINTS

1. As quoted in *History of Vatican II: Volume I: Announcing and Preparing Vatican Council II Toward a New Era in Catholicism*, ed. Giuseppe Alberigo and Joseph Komonchak (Maryknoll, NY: Orbis, and Leuven: Peeters, 1995), 15. Alberigo cites from the pope's own text of the speech and not the official version, which is heavily edited.

2. See *History of Vatican II: Volume I*, chapter 2.

3. Other rites are many in the Catholic Church. They include those of the Eastern rite Catholic churches, ritual usages particular to certain religious families, such as the Carmelites or Dominicans, and rites special to the place where they arose historically, such as the Ambrosian rite, which is celebrated in Milan.

4. There is no notion of preserving the Tridentine usage as a "separate rite" implied here.

5. Odo Casel, *The Mystery of Christian Worship and Other Writings*, ed. Burkhard Neunheuser, OSB (Westminster, MD: The Newman Press, 1962).

6. Louis Bouyer, *The Liturgy Revived* (Notre Dame: University of Notre Dame Press, 1964) 32.

7. Josef Jungmann, in *Commentary on the Documents of Vatican II, Volume I*, ed. Herbert Vorgrimler (New York: Herder and Herder, 1967), 12. See footnotes 12 and 13 to the constitution. Quotes were taken from the Easter Preface and an oration from the Easter Vigil in the Missal of 1570.

8. Theodore of Mopsuestia, "Instructions to Candidates for Baptism," in *Documents of the Baptismal Liturgy*, ed. E. C. Whitaker (London: SPCK, 1960), 45.

9. William Harmless, *Augustine and the Catechumenate* (Collegeville, MN: Liturgical Press, 1995), 365.

10. Raniero Cantalamessa, *The Mystery of Easter* (Collegeville, MN: Liturgical Press, 1993), 17.

11. Jungmann, 13.

12. Cf. Saint Jerome's dictum: "Ignorance of the Scriptures is ignorance of Christ."

13. Jungmann, 34–35.

14. The notion of limbo has never been a part of the church's official teaching, but is rather a theological opinion. The idea has fallen out of favor in the present era, and was actually rejected by the International Theological Commission in 2006.

15. Bede, *A History of the English Church and People*, I, 27, II, trans. Leo Sherly-Price (Baltimore: Penguin Books, 1955), 72–73.

16. Paradoxically, the printing press also made available for study a wide variety of texts in which the diversity of the tradition can be discovered.

17. Paul Turner, *The Hallelujah Highway: A History of the Catechumenate* (Chicago: Liturgy Training Publications, 2000), chapters 24–30.

18. As cited in Jacques Dourne, *God Loves the Pagans: A Christian Mission on the Plateaux of Vietnam*, trans. Rosemary Sheed (New York, Herder and Herder, 1966), 116.

19. Jungmann, 52.

20. Ibid., 21.

21. For example, Johannes Brinktrine, in *La Santa Messa* (Rome, 1952), 279, layers spurious theological claims upon a practice whose roots were completely elsewhere: "The 'beginning' is read at the end of the Mass because its lofty contents, the Incarnation of the Son of God, stand in strict relation with the mystery which is unfolded in the celebration of the Sacrifice." Quoted in Annibale Bugnini, *The Simplification of the Rubrics* (Collegeville, MN: Doyle and Finegan, 1955), 114.

22. For an opposing view, see Alcuin Reid, OSB, *The Organic Development of the Liturgy: The Principles of the Liturgical Reform and Their Relation to the Twentieth Century Liturgical Movement Prior to the Second Vatican Council* (Hants: Saint Michael's Abbey Press, 2004), 162–63. Following Capelle, he asserts that the renewal of baptism is sufficiently expressed by taking communion. He takes no account of the *Pascha Annotinum*, and thus deems the practice "totally novel."

23. Pierre Jounel, in *Voices from the Council*, ed. Michael R. Prendergast and M. D. Ridge (Portland, OR: Pastoral Press, 2004), 164.

24. Jungmann, 24–25.

25. Rembert G. Weakland, "Liturgy and Common Ground," *America* 180:5 (February 20, 1999): 7–11. See also Burkhard Neunheuser, OSB, "Roman Genius Revisited" in *Liturgy for the New Millennium: A Commentary on the Revised Sacramentary*, ed. Mark R. Francis and Keith F. Pecklers (Collegeville, MN: Liturgical Press, 2000), 35–48. For the most recent edition of Bishop's essay, see *Ephemerides Liturgicae* 110 (1996), 428–42, ed. Cuthbert Johnson and Jeremy Ward.

26. For more information about the controversy over this issue up until Vatican II, see Keith F. Pecklers, SJ, *Dynamic Equivalence: The Living Language of Christian Worship* (Collegeville, MN: Liturgical Press, 2003).

27. Columba Kelly, in *Voices from the Council*, 274.

28. Pierre Jounel, 1994 interview, in *Voices from the Council*, 161–62.

29. Jungmann, 41–42.

30. This provision sought to change what had been taught previously, namely, that to fulfill one's Sunday obligation, Catholics need only be present for the offertory, the canon of the Mass, and the priest's communion. The constitution, by asserting that the Liturgy of the Word and the Liturgy of the

Eucharist are so closely linked that they form "one single act of worship" (*SC*, 56), created a different standard.

PART III: IMPLEMENTATION

1. A notable conservative participant at the council was the French archbishop, Marcel Lefèbvre. At the time of the council he was archbishop of Dakar, Senegal, and member of the Spiritan congregation, a missionary religious community. He subsequently left the Spiritans. He founded a seminary in Ecône, Switzerland, and the Priestly Society of Saint Pius X, to perpetuate a form of Catholicism opposed in a number of respects to the teachings of the Second Vatican Council. Lefèbvre and his followers formally broke with Rome when he illicitly ordained four bishops in 1988.

2. The acclamation in question is the one that appears after "... the mystery of faith." The people respond: "Christ has died..." or "When we eat this bread..." or "Dying, you destroyed our death..." or "Lord, by your cross and resurrection...." It is called the memorial acclamation.

3. The epiclesis is also described as a "split epiclesis" because it calls down the Spirit twice: once over the elements and once over the people. The use of a split epiclesis has occasioned some criticism by liturgical scholars.

4. Otto Nussbaum, *Der Standort des Liturgen am christlichen Altar vor dem Jahre 1000. Eine archäologische und liturgiegeschichtliche Untersuchung* (Hanstein, 1965).

5. Gerald A. Arbuckle, *Violence, Society, and the Church: A Cultural Approach* (Collegeville, MN: Liturgical Press, 2004), chapter 7.

6. Annibale Bugnini, *The Reform of the Liturgy: 1948–1975* (Collegeville, MN: Liturgical Press, 1990), 269–76.

7. For many parishes, the communal service has been associated only with the seasons of Advent and Lent, a limitation not found in the rite itself.

8. *Journey to the Fullness of Life*, (Washington, DC: USCCB Publishing, 2000).

9. In addition, there were two unclear responses that the authors of the study took to be negative.

10. CARA Seminary Forum, *A Survey Report on the Teaching and Celebration of Liturgy*, September 1974.

11. Congregation for Catholic Education, *Instruction on Liturgical Formation in Seminaries* (Rome: Typis Polyglottis Vaticanis, 1979).

12. Nathan Mitchell, "Liturgical Education in Roman Catholic Seminaries: A Report and an Appraisal," *Worship* 54 (1980): 129–57.

13. Rembert G. Weakland, "Liturgical Renewal: Two Latin Rites?" *America* 176:20 (June 7–14, 1997): 13.

14. Cardinal Joseph Cordeiro, "The Liturgy Constitution, *Sacrosanctum Concilium,*" in *Vatican II Revisited by Those Who Were There*, ed. Alberic Stacpoole (Minneapolis: Winston Press, 1986), 189.

15. Weakland, "Liturgical Renewal: Two Latin Rites?" 14.

16. John Page, "The Process of Revision of the Sacramentary: 1981–1998," in *Liturgy for the New Millennium: A Commentary on the Revised Sacramentary*, ed. Mark R. Francis and Keith F. Pecklers (Collegeville, MN: Liturgical Press, 2000), 8.

17. "Changes at the top of ICEL herald new approaches on liturgy," *The Tablet* (August 17, 2002): 19–21.

18. Page, 12.

19. "New texts composed in a vernacular language . . . are to contain nothing that is inconsistent with the function, meaning, structure, style, theological content, traditional vocabulary or other important qualities of the texts found in the *editiones typicae*" (*LA*, 107). It is hard to imagine a text that could meet all of these criteria yet be "new."

20. "Some Aspects of the Church Understood as Communion," *Origins* 12:7 (June 25, 1992): 108.

21. Horace T. Allen, Jr., "Common Lectionary and Protestant Hymnody: Unity at the Table of the Word—Liturgical and Ecumenical Bookends," in *Liturgical Renewal as a Way to Christian Unity*, ed. James F. Puglisi (Collegeville, MN: Liturgical Press, 2005), 68.

22. See Robert F. Taft, SJ, "Mass Without the Consecration? The Historic Agreement on the Eucharist Between the Catholic Church and the Assyrian Church of the East Promulgated 26 October 2001," in *Liturgical Renewal as a Way to Christian Unity*, 199–224.

23. "Bishops pour cold water on new Mass translation," *The Tablet* (May 8, 2004): 42.

24. Cindy Wooden, "L.A. cardinal says Order of the Mass draft needs major work," Catholic News Service, May 12, 2004, 1.

25. Most Rev. Donald Trautman, "The Church's Ritual Books Since the Council: The Lectionary," *Today's Liturgy* (November 27, 2005–February 28, 2006): 14.

26. Mark R. Francis, CSV, "Overview of *Inculturation and the Roman Liturgy*," in *The Liturgy Documents: A Parish Resource, Volume Two* (Chicago: Liturgy Training Publications, 1999) 110.

27. Cf. *Inter Oecumenici*, 6; my translation.

28. Burkhard Neunheuser, OSB, "Roman Genius Revisited," in *Liturgy for the New Millennium*, 46.

29. Pope John Paul II, *Mane Nobiscum Domine*, 8; cf. *Novo Millenio Ineunte*, 35.

30. M. Francis Mannion, "Agendas for Liturgical Reform," *America* 175:17 (November 30, 1996): 9–16. The ideas the article contains were also presented in a scholarly lecture at the Center for Faith and Culture at Westminster College, Oxford, and published under the title "The Catholicity of the Liturgy: Shaping a New Agenda," in the book *Beyond the Prosaic: Renewing the Liturgical Movement*, ed. Strateford Caldecott (Edinburgh: T&T Clark, 1998), 11–48. This essay was reprinted in a collection of Mannion's essays, *Masterworks of God* (Chicago/Mundelein: Hillenbrand Books, 2004), under that same title.

31. Klaus Gamber, *The Reform of the Roman Liturgy: Its Problems and Background*, trans. Klaus D. Grimm (San Juan Capistrano, CA: Una Voce Press, 1993), 113.

32. Ibid., 113–14.

33. Ibid., 60.

34. Ibid.

35. Ibid., 91.

36. Quoted in "Testimonial by Msgr. Wilhelm Nyssen," Gamber, xiii.

37. *The Encyclopedia of American Religions: Volume 1*, ed. J. Gordon Melton (Tarrytown, NY: Triumph Books, 1991), 91, 93.

38. *Annuarium Statisticum Ecclesiae: Published for 2000*, L'Osservatore Romano Weekly Edition in English, May 15, 2002, page 8.

39. Aidan Nichols, OP, *Looking at the Liturgy: A Critical View of Its Contemporary Form* (San Francisco: Ignatius Press, 1996), 119–22.

40. Pope John Paul II, *Apostolic Letter on the 25th Anniversary of the Promulgation of the Conciliar Constitution* Sacrosanctum Concilium *on the Sacred Liturgy*, 12.

41. Ibid.

42. Pope John Paul II, *Ecclesia de Eucharistia*, 10.

43. "Signs continue to accumulate that the 'liturgy wars' in the Catholic Church are nearing an end.... The advocates of a more traditional, 'sacral' approach have won, while those who want a more flexible and idiomatic style of speech and worship have largely retreated..." John Allen, "Cardinal Pell and Vox Clara," *National Catholic Reporter* 3:30 (March 19, 2004); The Word from Rome Archives, <NCROnline.org>.

44. Peter Steinfels observes this phenomenon in his book *A People Adrift* (New York: Simon and Schuster [2003], 178–80). He highlights some woeful comments made by Sr. Kathleen Hughes, a liturgical scholar and contemporary American proponent of liturgical renewal, in her book *Saying Amen: A Mystagogy of Sacrament* (Chicago: Liturgy Training Publications [1999], xi–xx). Hughes is writing to oppose a "reform of the reform" (xi), but in fact grants

several of the premises of those who advocate such a course, including the charge that "reformed rites do not appear to have made an appreciable difference in contemporary church life..." (xx).

PART IV: THE STATE OF THE QUESTIONS

1. *Voices from the Council*, ed. Michael R. Prendergast and M. D. Ridge (Portland, OR: Pastoral Press, 2004).

2. A few persons were not asked the question. Of those asked, only two said yes: Archbishop Denis Hurley of Durban, South Africa, and Archbishop Emeritus Augusto Trujillo Arango of Tunja in Colombia.

3. Society of Saint Pius X, *The Problem of the Liturgical Reform: A Theological and Liturgical Study* (Kansas City, MO: Angelus Press, 2001) Part II.

4. *Vicesimus Quintus Annus* (4 December 1988), 21; *Spiritus et Sponsa* (4 December 2003), 12; and *Mane Nobiscum Domine* (October 2004–October 2005), 17.

5. David Regan, CSSp, *Experience the Mystery: Pastoral Possibilities for Christian Mystagogy* (Collegeville, MN: Liturgical Press, 1994), chapter 2.

6. <http://www.vatican.va/roman_curia/synod/documents/rc_synod_doc_20040528_lineamenta-xi-assembly_en.html>. Unfortunately, the chapter was somewhat confused. It claimed, oddly, that although a sense of mystery persists in the modern world, the basic problem lies in rejection of our capacity to know God through *reason* (no. 46). It lauded the method of typology used by the church fathers (no. 45), but at the same time advised that mystagogy be left to the Spirit and that it "must avoid an exaggerated use of symbolism...[and] lengthy, drawn out commentary" (no. 47). Quite a few topics included in the chapter seemed to be related to reverence (the donning of vestments, the layout of churches, the orientation of worship), but their relation to mystagogy was not explained. Finally, no distinctions were made among the various kinds of mystagogy or the diverse settings in which they might arise. Although the chapter contained many individual statements that seemed quite sensible, the overall effect on reading it was similar to that of reading notes from a brainstorming session before clarity or consensus has been reached.

7. Rates of attendance are measured differently by various studies. The Center for Applied Research in the Apostolate, at Georgetown University, offers several: <http://cara.georgetown.edu/bulletin/index.htm>. All show less than 50 percent attendance on average, even when the studies are limited to those countries with the highest percentages of Catholics.

8. Recent attempts to get at this subject, such as the essay of John Baldovin, SJ, "Why Go to Mass?" (*America* 190:16 [May 10, 2004]: 13–15; the

piece is taken from his book, *Bread of Life, Cup of Salvation: Understanding the Mass*, published by Sheed & Ward in 2003) are encouraging. Without explicitly using the council's language, the ten reasons he gives nonetheless richly illustrate how the liturgy does indeed serve as "summit and source."

9. Cardinal Joseph Ratzinger (Pope Benedict XVI), *The Spirit of the Liturgy*, trans. John Saward (San Francisco: Ignatius Press, 2000), 172 ff.

10. See also Pope Paul VI, *Ecclesiam Suam*.

11. For an interesting first-person account of how this event took shape, see the interview with Father James Chukwuma Okoye, CSSp, "Out of Africa," *Spiritan* 30:1 (Toronto, ON, February 2006) 10.

12. John Mansford Prior, SVD, "Inculturation of worship and spirituality —A view from Indonesia" <http://www.sedos.org/english/mansford.htm>.

13. Ibid.

14. Ibid.

15. See, for example, "Liturgy and Inculturation" in *Handbook for Liturgical Studies, Volume II: Fundamental Liturgy* (Collegeville, MN: Liturgical Press, 1998), 337–75; *Liturgical Inculturation: Sacramentals, Religiosity, and Catechesis* (Collegeville, MN: Liturgical Press, 1992); *Shaping the Easter Feast* (Washington, DC: Pastoral Press, 1992); and *Liturgies of the Future: The Process and Methods of Inculturation* (Mahwah, NJ: Paulist Press, 1989).

16. As examples of the former, he notes the Ndzon Melen Eucharistic Rite in Cameroon (1969) and the Zaire Mass (1973; approved by Rome in 1988); of the latter, the Liturgy of Second Burial of the Shona people in Zimbabwe (approved by the bishops of Zimbabwe in 1982). Aylward Shorter, "Inculturation of African Traditional Religious Values in Christianity—How Far?" <http://www.afrikaworld.net/afrel/shorter.htm>.

17. Synodus Episcoporum Bulletin, XI Ordinary General Assembly of The Synod Of Bishops, 2–23 October 2005, *The Eucharist: Source and Summit of the Life and Mission of the Church*, [00187-02.03] [IN146], October 10, 2005.

18. Between 1978 and 2000, the church in Africa grew 137.4 percent. During that same period, the Catholic Church. in Asia experienced a growth of 69.4 percent. *Annuarium Statisticum Ecclesiae: Published for 2000*, L'Osservatore Romano Weekly Edition in English, May 15, 2002.

19. For the reform of the liturgical books, see Annibale Bugnini, *The Reform of the Liturgy: 1948–1975*, trans. Matthew J. O'Connell (Collegeville, MN: Liturgical Press, 1990); for developments in music, see J. Michael Joncas, *From Sacred Music to Ritual Song: Twentieth Century Understandings of Roman Catholic Worship Music* (Collegeville, MN: Liturgical Press, 1997); for sacred art and architecture, see R. Kevin Seasoltz, *A Sense of the Sacred* (Collegeville, MN: Liturgical Press, 2005) and Michael E. DeSanctis, *Building from Belief: Advance, Retreat, and Compromise in the Remaking of Catholic Church Architecture* (Collegeville, MN:

Liturgical Press, 2005); and, for the Liturgy of the Hours, see Stanislaus Campbell, FSC, *From Breviary to Liturgy of the Hours: The Structural Reform of the Roman Office, 1964–1971* (Collegeville, MN: Liturgical Press, 1995).

20. Pierre-Marie Gy, OP, in *Voices from the Council*, 156.

21. Synodus Episcoporum Bulletin, XI Ordinary General Assembly of The Synod Of Bishops, 2–23 October 2005, *The Eucharist: Source and Summit of the Life and Mission of the Church*, [00148-02.02] [IN105], October 10, 2005.

22. Bishop Robert Lynch, "The Bishop and the Liturgy in Parishes," *Origins* 34:25 (December 2, 2004) 399–403.

23. Another survey conducted by the Federation of Diocesan Liturgical Commissions in 2003, devoted to the experience of priests within ten years of their ordination, collected information concerning their liturgical formation, such as the perceived strengths and weakness of the formation received, and the level of satisfaction of the priests themselves.

24. Between 1978 and 2000, the number of permanent deacons increased by 400.25 percent worldwide. Between 1990 and 2000 alone, the number of "lay missionaries" (lay pastoral workers who are neither members of secular institutes nor catechists) increased by 4,470.2 percent, and catechists rose by 48 percent. *Annuarium Statisticum Ecclesiae:* Published for 2000, L'Osservatore Romano Weekly Edition in English, May 15, 2002.

25. I am indebted to Philip Swoboda for this expression.

PART V

FURTHER READING

The Liturgical Movement

Botte, OSB, Bernard. *From Silence to Participation: An Insider's View of Liturgical Renewal*, translated by John Sullivan, OCD. Washington, DC: The Pastoral Press, 1988. This is an invaluable and engaging memoir by one of the most influential liturgical scholars of the twentieth century.

Crichton, J. D. *As It Was: Reminiscences and Prophecies.* Mildenhall, Suffolk: Decani Books, 1999. One of the leading British voices of the liturgical movement reflects on his lifelong engagement with the work of reform and renewal.

Fenwick, John R. K., and Bryan Spinks. *Worship in Transition: The Liturgical Movement in the Twentieth Century.* New York: Continuum, 1995. A study of how the liturgical change has taken place in all the major Christian denominations around the globe during the twentieth century.

How Firm a Foundation: Leaders of the Liturgical Movement. Compiled by Robert L. Tuzik. Chicago: Liturgy Training Publications, 1990. This volume, a companion to the one by Hughes (below), has a chronology up to 1989. A long list of Americans is included.

How Firm a Foundation: Voices of the Early Liturgical Movement. Compiled by Kathleen Hughes, RSCJ. Chicago: Liturgy Training Publications, 1990. This collection of excerpts from primary sources includes brief biographical introductions identifying each author.

Pecklers, SJ, Keith. *The Unread Vision: The Liturgical Movement in the United States of America: 1926–1955.* Collegeville, MN: Liturgical Press, 1998. The distinctive contributions of key Americans are set in the context of the worldwide movement.

————. *Dynamic Equivalence: The Living Language of Christian Worship.* Collegeville, MN: Liturgical Press, 2003. The story of the movement to establish worship in the vernacular before, during, and after the council.

Reid, OSB, Alcuin. *The Organic Development of the Liturgy: The Principles of Liturgical Reform and Their Relation to the Twentieth-Century Liturgical Movement Prior to the Second Vatican Council.* San Francisco: Ignatius Press, 2005. A detailed scholarly study in which the author argues that most of the reforms of the twentieth century are not in keeping with sound principles.

The Sacerdotal Communities of Saint-Severin of Paris and Saint-Joseph of Nice. *The Liturgical Movement. New York: Hawthorne Books, 1964.* A brief summary of the worldwide movement up to the time of the council.

The Constitution

Alberigo, Giuseppe, and Joseph Komonchak, editors. *History of Vatican II.* Maryknoll, NY: Orbis, and Leuven: Peeters, 1995–2006, five volumes. This series contains a wealth of recent research. The volumes are arranged in chronological order; volumes one and two are the most relevant to the Constitution on the Sacred Liturgy.

Bouyer, Louis. *The Liturgy Revived.* Notre Dame: University of Notre Dame Press, 1964. This brief and insightful reflection highlights some of the major themes of the document.

Crichton, J. D. *The Church's Worship: Considerations on the Liturgical Constitution of the Second Vatican Council.* New York: Sheed & Ward, 1964. This commentary also includes consideration of the first instruction on the implementation of the constitution, *Inter Oecumenici.*

Gil Hellín, Francisco. *Concilii Vaticani II synopsis in ordinem redigens schemata cum relationibus necnon Patrum orationes atque animadversiones: Constitutio de Sacra Liturgia Sacrosanctum concilium.* Vatican City: Libreria Editrice Vaticana, 2003. A presentation of the four successive drafts of *Sacrosanctum Concilium* in parallel columns with an appendix of all the written and oral observations by the council fathers. The book is entirely in Latin, except for a brief introduction in Italian, Spanish, and English.

Jackson, Pamela. *An Abundance of Graces: Reflections on Sacrosanctum Concilium.* Chicago/Mundelein: Hillenbrand Books, 2004. In addition to the author's comments, complete texts in English of *Tra le Sollecitudini, Mediator Dei,* and *Sacrosanctum Concilium* are included in the back of the book.

Marini, Piero. *Sacrosanctum Concilium: Memoria di una esperienza vissuta nelle celebrazioni liturgiche del santo padre.* Vatican City: Libreria Editrice Vaticana, 2004. A memoir and reflection on the lasting importance of the constitution, the work ends with a call to confidence in the future of this irreversible reform of the liturgy. Archbishop Marini served under Pope Paul VI as secretary to Archbishop Bugnini from 1965–75, and has been papal master of ceremonies from 1987 to the present. In Italian.

Vorgrimler, Herbert, editor. *Commentary on the Documents of Vatican II.* New York: Herder and Herder, 1967. Volume I contains a very valuable commentary on each article of the Constitution on the Sacred Liturgy by Josef Jungmann, SJ, a peritus at the council.

Reforms Following the Council

The Awakening Church: 25 Years of Liturgical Renewal. Edited by Lawrence J. Madden. Collegeville, MN: Liturgical Press, 1992. This collection of essays came out of a symposium gathered to assess the effectiveness of efforts at liturgical renewal after the council. All the participants respond to survey data from parishes deemed exemplary.

Boyer, Mark G. *The Liturgical Environment: What the Documents Say, 2nd Edition.* Collegeville, MN: Liturgical Press, 2004. This book synthesizes a great number of post-conciliar church documents concerning art, environment, and artifacts of the liturgy.

Bugnini, Annibale. *The Reform of the Liturgy: 1948–1975,* translated by Matthew J. O'Connell. Collegeville, MN: Liturgical Press, 1990. An invaluable account of the reform of the liturgy in all its aspects, including detailed discussions of individual reforms, and lists of those who worked on the various committees. The scope of the book includes earlier liturgical reforms and an account of what happened at the council, but its greatest contribution is to the question of how the reforms after the council took shape.

Campbell, FSC, Stanislaus. *From Breviary to Liturgy of the Hours: The Structural Reform of the Roman Office, 1964–1971.* Collegeville, MN: Liturgical Press, 1995. A detailed scholarly study of the reform of the Liturgy of the Hours.

Chupungco, OSB, Anscar. *Liturgical Inculturation: Sacramentals, Religiosity, and Catechesis.* Collegeville, MN: Liturgical Press, 1992. This book looks at catechesis and various aspects of Christian piety and their effects on liturgical celebration.

————. *Liturgies of the Future: The Process and Methods of Inculturation.* Mahwah, NJ: Paulist Press, 1989. A clear overall presentation of the topic of liturgical inculturation from a leading scholar in this field.

Collins, Mary. *Contemplative Participation: Sacrosanctum Concilium Twenty-five Years Later.* Collegeville, MN: Liturgical Press, 1990. A brief reflection on the state of the questions by a liturgy scholar from the Catholic University of America.

DeSanctis, Michael E. *Building from Belief: Advance, Retreat, and Compromise in the Remaking of Catholic Church Architecture.* Collegeville, MN: Liturgical Press, 2002. Written for a popular audience, this work illustrates how attitudes and beliefs are embodied in the principles of art and architecture that have arisen from the council.

Elavathingal, Sebastian. *Inculturation and Christian Art: An Indian Perspective*. Rome: Urbania University Press, 1990. This scholarly work gives a fine in-depth example of what the process of inculturation can mean for Christian art.

"The Faithful Revolution," Video Documentary. Allen, TX: Resources for Christian Living, 1997. A series of five videocassettes about Vatican II, grouped thematically.

Full, Active, and Conscious Participation: Celebrating Twenty-Five Years of Today's Liturgy. Edited by Michael R. Prendergast. Portland, OR: Pastoral Press, 2003. A collection of popular articles about liturgical praxis since the reform, from the magazine of Oregon Catholic Press.

Gamber, Klaus. *The Reform of the Roman Liturgy: Its Problems and Background*. Translated by Klaus D. Grimm. Harrison, NY: Una Voce Press, 1993. This book offers a generally negative portrayal of most of the reforms since the council. Written for a popular audience, it also includes a question and answer section.

Handbook for Liturgical Studies, five volumes. Edited by Anscar Chupungco, OSB. Collegeville, MN: Liturgical Press, 1998. Although not framed as an account of Vatican II, the reforms of the council are a reference point for the topics contained in these volumes.

Jeffrey, Peter. "A Chant Historian Reads *Liturgiam Authenticam* 1: The Latin Liturgical Traditions," *Worship* 78:1 (January 2004) 2–24; "A Chant Historian Reads *Liturgiam Authenticam* 2: The Bible and the Roman Rite," *Worship* 78:2 (March 2004) 139–64; "A Chant Historian Reads *Liturgiam Authenticam* 3: Languages and Cultures," *Worship* 78:3 (May 2004) 236–65; "A Chant Historian Reads *Liturgiam Authenticam* 4: Human and Angelic Tongues," *Worship* 78:4 (July 2004) 309–41. This four-part study discusses in depth the problematic nature of the directives set forth in the instruction *Liturgiam Authenticam*, when viewed in light of liturgical history.

Joncas, J. Michael. *From Sacred Song to Ritual Music: Twentieth-Century Understandings of Roman Catholic Worship Music*. Collegeville, MN:

Liturgical Press, 1997. A systematic presentation of the development of ideas about church music from 1903 to 1997, as seen through Roman documents, national documents (U.S.), the Milwaukee Report, and the Snowbird Statement.

Kabasele Lumbala, François. *Celebrating Jesus Christ in Africa: Liturgy and Inculturation.* Maryknoll, NY: Orbis Books, 1998. This book addresses the inculturation of all the sacraments and rites of the Catholic Church in Africa, raising challenging questions that can be asked more broadly.

Kavanagh, Aidan. *The Shape of Baptism: The Rite of Christian Initiation.* New York: Pueblo Publishing Company, 1978. This profound and insightful work includes discussion of the origins and reform of baptism and the restoration of the catechumenate called for by the council.

Liturgical Renewal as a Way to Christian Unity. Edited by James F. Puglisi. Collegeville, MN: Liturgical Press, 2005. This book of scholarly essays by contributors from various Christian communities grew out of a series of conferences held at the ecumenical research center, Centro Pro Unione, in Rome.

Liturgy for the New Millennium: A Commentary on the Revised Sacramentary. Edited by Mark R. Francis, CSV, and Keith F. Pecklers, SJ. Collegeville, MN: Liturgical Press, 2000. A collection of essays by liturgical scholars. Although the title highlights the revised Sacramentary (which has not appeared in English as of this writing), the essays cover a variety of topics concerning liturgical renewal and revision.

Mannion, M. Francis. *Masterworks of God: Essays in Liturgical Theory and Practice.* Chicago/Mundelein: Hillenbrand Books, 2004. A collection of two decades of critical essays by the leader of the contemporary movement to "recatholicize the reform."

Marini, Piero. *Liturgia e Bellezza, Nobilis Pulchritudo: Memoria di una esperienza vissuta nelle celebrazioni liturgiche del santo padre.* Vatican City: Libreria Editrice Vaticana, 2005. This fine work includes the author's earlier book, cited above. It has been expanded, however, to include a second section that describes how the papal liturgy has been reformed in the years since the council and according to its principles. In Italian. See also this text by the author, in English, on the Vatican Web site: <http://212.77.1.245/news_services/liturgy/2004/documents/ns_lit_doc _20040202_liturgia-bellezza_en.html>.

Nichols, OP, Aidan. *Looking at the Liturgy: A Critical View of Its Contemporary Form.* San Francisco: Ignatius Press, 1996. The author adduces findings from recent anthropological studies to support his critique of the reformed liturgy. The book is a call to action, and ends with the author's recommendations.

Ratzinger, Cardinal Joseph (Pope Benedict XVI). *The Spirit of the Liturgy.* Translated by John Saward. San Francisco: Ignatius Press, 2001. A theologian's view of the issues implicit in several key areas of liturgical practice. The title of the book gives homage to Romano Guardini.

Seasoltz, R. Kevin. *A Sense of the Sacred.* Collegeville, MN: Liturgical Press, 2005. This broad history of sacred art and architecture also provides context from the history of secular architecture and art. It ends with a discussion of examples, both successful and less so, from the post-conciliar period.

Society of Saint Pius X. *The Problem of the Liturgical Reform: A Theological and Liturgical Study.* Kansas City, MO: Angelus Press, 2001. This study argues that the reformed liturgy strays dangerously far from Catholic orthodoxy, and that the Mass of Pius V uniquely represents authentic Catholic tradition.

Vatican II Assessment and Perspectives: Twenty-five Years After, 3 volumes. Edited by René Latourelle. Mahwah, NJ: Paulist Press, 1988–89. The authors reflect on all aspects of the council, including the liturgical renewal it engendered.

Vatican II Revisited by Those Who Were There. Edited by Alberic Stacpoole. Minneapolis: Winston Press, 1986. These essays contain indepth discussions of issues as well as personal recollections about how the work of the council took shape and how it has been received in the intervening years.

Voices from the Council. Edited by Michael Prendergast and M. D. Ridge. Portland, OR: Pastoral Press, 2004. This collection of thirty-three interviews or essays, although a bit uneven, contains some fine observations and insights about the council and its influence. Bishops, *periti,* observers, and others are included.

White, James F. *Roman Catholic Worship: Trent to Today.* Collegeville, MN: Liturgical Press, 2003. This easily readable liturgical history examines transitions in worship within the context of cultural change. Three of its eight chapters are devoted to Vatican II.

INDEX